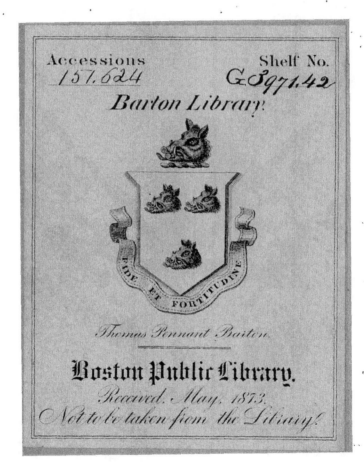

TIS
Pitty Shee's a Whore

Acted by the *Queenes* Maiesties Seruants, at *The Phænix* in
Drury-Lane.

LONDON,
Printed by *Nicholas Okes* for *Richard*
Collins, and are to be fold at his fhop
in *Pauls* Church-yard, at the figne
of the three Kings. 1633.

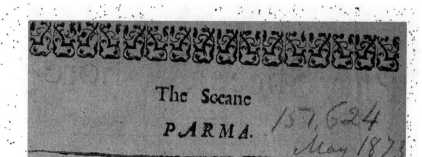

The Sceane
PARMA.

The Actors Names.

Bonauentura,	A Fryar.
A Cardinall,	Nuntio to the Pope.
Soranzo,	A Nobleman.
Florio,	A Cittizen of *Parma.*
Donado,	Another Cittizen.
Grimaldi,	A Roman Gentleman.
Giouanni,	Sonne to *Florio.*
Bergetto,	Nephew to *Donado.*
Richardetto,	A suppos'd Phisitian.
Vasques,	Seruant to *Soranzo.*
Poggio,	Seruant to *Bergetto.*
Bandetti,	

Woemen.

Annabella,	Daughter to *Florio.*
Hippolita,	Wife to *Richardetto.*
Philotis,	His Neece.
Putana,	Tutresse to *Annabella.*

To the truely Noble, *John*, Earle of *Peterborough*, Lord Mordant, Baron of *Turuey*.

My LORD,

Here a Truth of *Meritt* hath a generall warrant, There *Loue* is but *a Debt, Acknowledgement a Iustice*. Greatnesse cannot often claime *Virtue* by Inheritance ; Yet in this, YOVRS appeares most Eminent, for that you are not more rightly Heyre to your *Fortunes*, then Glory shalbe to your *Memory*. Sweetenesse of disposition ennobles a freedome of Birth ; in BOTH, your lawfull Interest adds Honour to your owne Name, and mercy to my presumption. Your Noble allowance of *These First Fruites* of my leasure in the Action, emboldens my confidence, of your as noble construction in this Presentment : especially since my Seruice must euer owe particular duty to your Fauours,

A 2   uours,

uours, by a particular Ingagement. The Grauity of the *Subiect* may eafily excuse the leightneffe of the *Title* : otherwife, I had beene a feuere Iudge againft mine owne guilt. Princes haue vouchfaft Grace to trifles, offred from a purity of Deuotion, your Lordfhip may likewife pleafe, to admit into your good opinion, with thefe weake endeuours, the conftancy of Affection from the fincere *Louer* of your Deferts in Honour.

IOHN FORD.

'Tis Pitty Shee's a
VVHOORE. *Witt Texius*

Enter Fryar *and* Giouanni.

Fryar.

Ifpute no more in this, for know (young man)
Thefe are no Schoole-points; nice Philofophy
May tolerate vnlikely arguments,
But Heauen admits no jeft; wits that prefum'd
On wit too much, by ftriuing how to proue
There was no God; with foolifh grounds of
Difcouer'd firft the neereft way to Hell; (Art,
And fild the world with deuelifh Atheifme:
Such queftions youth are fond; For better 'tis,
To bleffe the Sunne, then reafon why it fhines;
Yet hee thou talk'ft of, is aboue the Sun,
No more; I may not heare it.

  Gio. Gentle Father,
To you I haue vnclafp't my burthened foule,
Empty'd the ftore-houfe of my thoughts and heart,
Made my felfe poore of fecrets; haue not left
Another word vntold, which hath not fpoke
All what I euer durft, or thinke, or know;
And yet is here the comfort I fhall haue,
Muft I not doe, what all men elfe may, loue?
  Fry. Yes, you may loue faire fonne.
  Gio. Muft I not praife
That beauty, which if fram'd a new, the gods
Would make a god of, if they had it there;
And kneele to it, as I doe kneele to them?

     Fry.

Fry. Why foolish mad-man?

Gio. Shall a peeuish sound,
A cuſtomary forme, from man to man,
Of brother and of ſiſter, be a barre
Twixt my perpetuall happineſſe and mee?
Say that we had one father, ſay one wombe,
(Curſe to my ioyes) gaue both vs life, and birth;
Are wee not therefore each to other bound
So much the more by Nature; by the the links
Of blood, of reaſon; Nay if you will hau't,
Euen of Religion; to be euer one,
One ſoule, one fleſh, one loue, one heart, one *All*?

Fry. Haue done vnhappy youth, for thou art loſt.

Gio. Shall then, (for that I am her brother borne)
My ioyes be euer baniſht from her bed?
No Father; in your eyes I ſee the change
Of pitty and compaſſion: from your age
As from a ſacred *Oracle* diſtills
The life of Counſell: tell mee holy man,
What Cure ſhall giue me eaſe in theſe extreames.

Fry. Repentance (ſonne) and ſorrow for this ſinne:
For thou haſt mou'd a Maieſty aboue
With thy vn-raunged (almoſt) Blaſphemy.

Gio. O doe not ſpeake of that (deare Confeſſor)

Fry. Art thou (my ſonne) that miracle of Wit,
Who once within theſe three Moneths wert eſteem'd
A wonder of thine age, throughout *Bononia*?
How did the Vniuerſity applaud
Thy Gouerment, Behauiour, Learning, Speech,
Sweetneſſe, and all that could make vp a man?
I was proud of my Tutellage, and choſe
Rather to leaue my Bookes, then part with thee,
I did ſo: but the fruites of all my hopes
Are loſt in thee, as thou art in thy ſelfe.
O *Gionanni*: haſt thou left the Schooles
Of Knowledge, to conuerſe with Luſt and Death?
(For Death waites on thy Luſt) looke through the world,

And

And thou shalt see a thousand faces shine
More glorious, then this Idoll thou ador'st:
Leaue her, and take thy choyce, 'tis much lesse sinne,
Though in such games as those, they lose that winne.

  Gio. It were more ease to stop the *Ocean*
From floates and ebbs, then to disswade my vowes.

  Fry. Then I haue done, and in thy wilfull flames
Already see thy ruine; Heauen is iust,
Yet heare my counsell.

  Gio. As a voyce of life.

  Fry. Hye to thy Fathers house, there locke thee fast
Alone within thy Chamber, then fall downe
On both thy knees, and grouell on the ground:
Cry to thy heart, wash euery word thou vtter'st
In teares, (and if't bee possible) of blood:
Begge Heauen to cleanse the leprosie of Lust
That rots thy Soule, acknowledge what thou art,
A wretch, a worme, a nothing: weepe, sigh, pray
Three times a day, and three times euery night:
For seuen dayes space doe this, then if thou find'st
No change in thy desires, returne to me:
I'le thinke on remedy, pray for thy selfe
At home, whil'st I pray for thee here—— away,
My blessing with thee, wee haue neede to pray.

  Gio. All this I'le doe, to free mee from the rod
Of vengeance, else I'le sweare, my Fate's my God. *Exeunt.*

Enter Grimaldi *and* Vasques *ready to fight.*

  Vas. Come sir, stand to your tackling, if you proue *Crauen*,
I'le make you run quickly.

  Gri. Thou art no equall match for mee.

  Vas. Indeed I neuer went to the warres to bring home newes,
nor cannot play the Mountibanke for a meales meate, and sweare
I got my wounds in the field: see you these gray haires, they'le
not flinch for a bloody nose, wilt thou to this geere?

  Gri. Why slaue, think'st thou I'le ballance my reputation
B 2   with

With a Caſt-ſuite ; Call thy Maiſter, he ſhall know that I dare——

Vaſ. Scold like a Cot-queane (that's your Profeſſion) thou poore
ſhaddow of a Souldier, I will make thee know, my Maiſter keepes
Seruants, thy betters, in quality and performance ; Com'ſt thou to
fight or prate?

Gri. Neither with thee,
I am a Romaine. and a Gentleman, one that haue got
Mine honour with expence of blood.

Vaſ. You are a lying Coward, and a foole, fight, or by theſe Hilts
I'le kill thee——braue my Lord,— you'le fight.

Gri. Prouoake me not, for if thou doſt —— *They fight, Grimal.* hath the

Vaſ. Haue at you. *mal. hath the worſt.*

       Enter Florio, Donado, Soranzo.

Flo. What meaned theſe ſudden broyles ſo neare my dores?
Haue you not other places, but my houſe
To vent the ſpleene of your diſordered bloods?
Muſt I be haunted ſtill with ſuch vnreſt,
As not to eate, or ſleepe in peace at home?
Is this your loue *Grimaldi* ? Fie, t'is naught.

Do. And *Vaſques*, I may tell thee tis not well
To broach theſe quarrels, you are euer forward
In ſeconding contentions.

       Enter aboue Annabella *and* Putana.

Flo. What's the ground?

Sor. That with your patience Signiors, I'le reſolue:
This Gentleman, whom fame reports a ſouldier,
(For elſe I know not) riuals mee in loue:
To Signior *Florio's* Daughter ; to whoſe eares
He ſtill preferrs his ſuite to my diſgrace,
Thinking the way to recommend himſelfe,
Is to diſparage me in his report:
But know *Grimaldi*, though (may be) thou art
My equall in thy blood, yet this bewrayes
A lowneſſe in thy minde ; which wer't thou Noble
Thou would'ſt as much diſdaine, as I doe thee
For this vnworthineſſe ; and on this ground
I will'd my Seruant to correct this tongue,

Holding

Holding a man, fo bafe, no match for me.

Vaf. And had your fudda ne comming prevented vs, I had let
my Gentleman blood vnder the gilles; I fhould haue worin'd
you Sir, for running madde.

Gri. Ile be reueng'd *Soranzo.*

Vaf. On a difh of warme-broth to ftay your ftomack, doe
honeft Innocence, doe; fpone-meat is a wholefomer dyet then
a fpannifh blade.

Gri. remember this.

Sor. I feare thee not *Grimaldi,*   *Ex. Gri.*

Flo. My Lord *Soranzo,* this is ftrange to me,
Why you fhould ftorme, hauing my word engag'd:
Owing her heart, what nee e you doubt her eare?
Loofers may talke by law of any game.

Vaf. Yet the villaine of words, fignior *Florio* may be fuch,
As would make any vnfpleen'd Doue, Chollerick,
Blame not my Lord in this.

Flo. Be you more filent,
I would not for my wealth, my daughters loue
Should caufe the fpilling of one drop of blood.
Vafques put vp, let's end this fray in wine.   *Exeunt.*

Putana How like you this child? here's threatning challeng-
ing, quarrelling, and fighting, on euery fide, and all is for your
fake; you had neede looke to your felfe (*Chardge*) you'le be
ftolne away fleeping elfe fhortly.

Annabella: But (*Tutreffe*) fuch a life giues no content
To me, my thoughts are fixt on other ends;
Would you would leaue me.

Put. Leaue you? no maruaile elfe; leaue me, no leauing (Chardge)
This is loue outright, Indeede I blame you not, you haue
Choyce fit for the beft Lady in *Italy.*

Anna. Pray doe not talke fo much.

Put. Take the worft with the beft, there's *Grimaldi* the
fouldier a very well-timbred fellow: they fay he is a Roman,
Nephew to the Duke *Mount Ferratto,* they fay he did good feruice in the warrs againft the *Millanoys,* but faith (*Chardge*) I doe
not like him, and be for nothing, but for being a fouldier; one a-

mongft.

:mongſt twenty of your skirmiſhing Captaines; but haue ſome
pryuie mayme or other, that marres their ſtanding vpright, I like
him the worſe, hee crinckles ſo much in the hams; though hee
might ſerue, if their were no more men, yet hee's not the man I
wou'd chooſe.

Anna. Fye how thou prat'ſt.

Put. As I am a very woman, I like *Signiour Soranzo,* well;
hee is wiſe, and what is more, rich; and what is more then that,
kind, and what is more then all this, a Noble-man; ſuch a one were
I the faire *Annabella,* my ſelfe, I would wiſh and pray for: then
hee is bountifull; beſides hee is handſome, and, by my troth, I
thinke wholſome : (and that's newes in a gallant of three and
twenty.) liberall that I know: louing, that you know; and a man
ſure, elſe hee could neuer ha' purchaſt ſuch a good name, with
Hippolita the luſtie Widdow in her husbands life time: And
t'were but for that report (ſweet heart) would a were thine:
Commend a man for his qualities, but take a husband as he is a
plaine-ſufficient, *naked man*: ſuch a one is for your bed, and ſuch
a one is *Signior Soranzo* my life for't.

Anna. Sure the woman tooke her mornings Draught to ſoone.

Enter Bergetto *and* Poggio.

Put. But looke (ſweet heart,) looke what thinge comes now:
Here's another of your cyphers to fill vp the number:
Oh braue old Ape in a ſilken Coate, obſerue.

Ber. Did'ſt thou thinke *Poggio*, that I would ſpoyle my
New cloathes, and leaue my dinner to fight.

Pog. No Sir, I did not take you for ſo arrant a babie.

Ber. I am wyſer then ſo: for I hope *Poggio*, thou
Neuer heard'ſt of an elder brother, that was a Coxcomb,
Did ſt *Poggio*?

Pog. Neuer indeede Sir, as long as they had either land or
mony left them to inhe rit.

Ber. Is it poſſible *Poggio*? oh monſtruous! why Ile vndertake, with a handfull of ſiluer, to buy a headfull of wit at any
tyme, but ſirrah, I haue another purchaſe in hand, I ſhall haue
the wench my ne vnckle ſayes, I will but waſh my face, and
ſhift ſocks, and then haue at her yfaith----

Mar I.e

Marke my pace *Poggio.*

Pog. Sir I haue seene an Asse, and a Mule trot the Spannish rauin with a better grace, I know not how often.

Exeunt.

Anna. This Ideot haunts me too.

Put. I, I, he needes no discription, the rich *Magnifico,* that is below with your Father (*Chardge*) *Signior Donado* his Vnckle; for that he meanes to make this his Cozen a golden calfe, thinkes that you wil be a right *Isralite,* and fall downe to him presently: but I hope I haue tuterd you better.: they say a fooles-bable is a Ladies playfellow: yet you hauing wealth enough, you neede not cast vpon the dearth of flesh at any rate: hang him Innocent.

Enter Giouanni.

Anna. But see *Putana,* see: what blessed shape Of some cælestiall Creature now appeares? What man is hee, that with such sad aspect Walkes carelesse of him selfe?

Put. Where?

Anna. Looke below.

Put. Oh, 'tis your brother sweet—

Anna. Ha!

Put. 'Tis your brother.

Anna. Sure 'tis not hee, this is some woefull thinge Wrapt vp in griefe, some shaddow of a man. Alas hee beats his brest, and wipes his eyes Drown'd all in teares: me thinkes I heare him sigh. Lets downe *Putana,* and pertake the cause, I know my Brother in the Loue he beares me, Will not denye me partage in his sadnesse, My soule is full of heauinesse and feare.

Exit.

Gio. Lost, I am lost: my fates haue doom'd my death: The more I striue, I loue, the more I loue, The lesse I hope: I see my ruine, certaine. What Iudgement, or endeuors could apply To my incurable and restlesse wounds, I throughly haue examin'd, but in vaine: O that it were not in Religion sinne,

To make our loue a God, and worship it.
I haue euen wearied heauen with prayers, dryed vp
The spring of my continuall teares, euen steru'd
My veines with dayly fasts: what wit or Art
Could Counsaile, I haue practiz'd; but alas
I find all thefe but dreames, and old mens tales
To fright vnsteedy youth; I'me still the same,
Or I must speake, or burst; tis not I know,
My lust; but tis my fate that leads me on.
Keepe feare and low faint hearted shame with slaues,
Ile tell her, that I loue her, though my heart
Were rated at the price of that attempt.
Oh me! she comes.

    Enter Anna and Putana.

  Anna. Brother.

  Gio. If such a thing
As Courage dwell in men, (yee heauenly powers)
Now double all that vertue in my tongue.

  Anna. Why Brother, will you not speake to me?

  Gio. Yes; how d'ee Sister?

  Anna. Howsoeuer I am, me thinks you are not well.

  Put. Blesse vs why are you so sad Sir.

  Gio. Let me intreat you leaue vs a while, *Putana*,
Sister, I would be pryuate with you.

  Anna. With-drawe *Putana*

  Put. I will
If this were any other Company for her, I should thinke my ab-
sence an office of some credit; but I will leaue them together.

    Exit Putana.

  Gio. Come Sister lend your hand, let's walke together,
I hope you neede not blush to walke with mee,
Here's none but you and I.

  Anna. How's this?

  Gio. Faith I meane no harme.

  Anna. Harme?

  Gio. No good faith; how ist with'ee?

  Anna. I trust hee be not franticke.

I

I am very well brother.

Gio. Truft me but I am ficke, I feare fo fick,
'Twill coft my life.

Anna. Mercy forbid it: 'tis not fo I hope.

Gio. I thinke you loue me Sifter.

Anna. Yes you know, I doe.

Gio. I know't indeed ----y'are very faire.

Anna. Nay then I fee you haue a merry ficknelfe.

Gio. That's as it proues: they Poets faigne (I read)
That *Iuno* for her forehead did exceede
All other goddeffes: but I durft fweare,
Your forehead exceeds hers, as hers did theirs.

Anna. Troth this is pretty.

Gio. Such a paire of ftarres
As are thine eyes, would (like *Promethean* fire.)
(If gently glaun'ft) giue life to fenfelefle ftones.

Anna. Fie vpon'ee.

Gio. The Lilly and the Rofe moft fweetly ftrainge,
Vpon your dimpled Cheekes doe ftriue for change.
Such lippes would tempt a Saint; fuch hands as thofe
Would make an *Anchoret* Lafciuious.

Anna. D'ee mock mee, or flatter mee.

Gio. If you would fee a beauty more exact
Then Art can counterfit, or nature frame,
Looke in your glaffe, and there behold your owne.

Anna. O you are a trime youth.

Gio. Here.   *Offers his Dagger to her.*

Anna. What to doe.

Gio. And here's my breaft, ftrick home.
Rip vp my bofome, there thou fhalt behold
A heart, in which is writ the truth I fpeake.
Why ftand'ee?   *Anna.* Are you earneft?

Gio. Yes moft earneft.
You cannot loue?   *Anna.* Whom?

Gio. Me, my tortur'd foule
Hath felt affliction in the heate of Death.
O *Annabella* I am quite vndone.

The loue of thee (my fifter) and the view
Of thy immortall beauty hath vntun'd
All harmony both of my rest and life,
Why d'ee not ftrike?

  Anna. Forbid it my iuft feares,
If this be true, 'twere fitter I were dead.

   Gio. True *Annabella*; 'tis no time to eft,
I haue too long fuppreft the hidden flames
That almoft haue confum'd me; I haue fpent
Many a filent night in fighes and groanes,
Ran ouer all my thoughts, defpis'd my Fate,
Reafon'd againft the reafons of my loue,
Done all that fmooth'd-cheeke Vertue could aduife,
But found all booteleffe; 'tis my deftiny,
That you muft eyther loue, or I muft dye.

   Anna. Comes this in fadneffe from you?

   Gio. Let fome mifchiefe
Befall me foone, if I diffemble ought.

   Anna. You are my brother *Giouanni.*

   Gio. You,
My Sifter *Annabella*; I know this:
And could afford you inftance why to loue
So much the more for this; to which intent
Wife Nature firft in your Creation ment
To make you mine: elfe 't had beene finne and foule,
To fhare one beauty to a double foule.
Neereneffe in birth or blood, doth but perfwade
A neerer neereneffe in affection.
I haue askt Counfell of the holy Church,
Who tells mee I may loue you, and 'tis iuft,
That fince I may, I fhould; and will, yes will.
Muft I now liue, or dye?

   Anna. Liue, thou haft wonne
The field, and neuer fought; what thou haft vrg'd,
My captiue heart had long agoe refolu'd.
I blufh to tell thee, (but I'le tell thee now)
For euery figh that thou haft fpent for me,

                              I

I haue figh'd ten; for euery teare ſhed twenty:
And not ſo much for that I lou'd, as that
I durſt not ſay I lou'd; uor ſcarcely thinke it.

    Gio. Let not this Muſicke be a dreame(yee gods)
For pittie's-ſake I begge 'ee.

    Anna. On my knees,   *Shee kneeles.*
Brother, euen by our Mothers duſt, I charge you,
Doe not betray mee to your mirth or hate,
Loue mee, or kill me Brother.

    Gio. On my knees,   *He kneeles.*
Siſter, euen by my Mothers duſt I charge ycu,
Doe not betray mee to your mirth or hate,
Loue mee, or kill mee Siſter.

    Anna. You meane good ſooth then?

    Gio. In good troth I doe,
And ſo doe you I hope: ſay, I'm in earneſt:

    Anna. I'le ſwear't and I:

    Gio. And I, and by this kiſſe,   *Kiſſes her.*
(Once more, yet once more, now let's riſe, by this)
I would not change this minute for *Elyzium,*
What muſt we now doe?

    Anna. What you will.   *Gio.* Come then,
After ſo many teares as wee haue wept,
Let's learne to court in ſmiles. to kiſſe and ſleepe.   *Exeunt.*

         Enter Florio *and* Donado.

    Flo. Signior Donado, you haue ſayd enough,
I vnderſtand you, but would haue you know,
I will not force my Daughter 'gainſt her will.
You ſee I haue but two, a Sonne and Her;
And hee is ſo deuoted to his Booke,
As I muſt tell you true, I doubt his health:
Should he miſcarry, all my hopes rely
Vpon my Girle; as for worldly Fortune,
I am I thanke my Starres, bleſt with enough:
My Care is how to match her to her liking,
I would not haue her marry Wealth, but Loue,
And if ſhe like your Nephew, let him haue her,

               C 2   Here's

Here's all that I can fay.

Do. Sir you fay well,
Like a true father, and for my part, I
If the young folkes can like, (twixt you and me)
Will promife to affure my Nephew prefently,
Three thoufand *Florrens* yeerely during life,
And after I am dead, my whole eftate.

Flo. 'Tis a faire proffer fir, meane time your Nephew
Shall haue free paffage to commence his fuite;
If hee can thriue, hee fhall haue my confent,
So for this time I'le leaue you *Sigzior.*   *Exit.*

Do. Well,
Here's hope yet, if my Nephew would haue wit,
But hee is fuch another Dunce, I feare
Hee'le neuer winne the Wench; when I was young
I could haue done't yfaith, and fo fhall hee
If hee will learne of mee; and in good time
Hee comes himfelfe.

Enter Bergetto *and* Poggio.

Pog. How now *Bergetto,* whether away fo faft?

Ber. Oh Vnkle, I haue heard the ftrangeft newes that euer
came out of the Mynt, haue I not *Poggio?*

Pog. Yes indeede Sir.   *Do.* What newes *Bergetto?*

Ber. Why looke yee Vnkle? my Barber told me iuft now
that there is a fellow come to Towne, who vndertakes to make
a Mill goe without the mortall helpe of any water or winde,
onely with Sand-bags; and this fellow hath a ftrange Horfe, a
moft excellent beaft, I'le affure you Vnkle, (my Barber fayes)
whofe head to the wonder of all Chriftian people, ftands iuft behind where his tayle is, is't not true *Poggio?*

Pog. So the Barber fwore forfooth.

Do. And you are running hither? *Ber.* I forfooth Vnkle.

Do. Wilt thou be a Foole ftil? come fir, you fhall not goe,
you haue more mind of a Puppet-play, then on the bufineffe I
told y'ee: why thou great Baby, wu't neuer haue wit, wu't
make thy felfe a May-game to all the world?

Pog. Anfwere for your felfe Maifter.

                                                            Ber.

Ber. Why Vnkle, fhu'd I fit at home ftill, and not goe abroad to fee fafhions like other gallants?

Do. To fee hobby-horfes what wife talke I pray had you with *Annabella*, when you were at *Signior Florio's* houfe?

Ber. Oh the wench: vds fa'me, Vnkle, I tickled her with a rare fpeech, that I made her almoft burft her belly with laughing.

Do. Nay I thinke fo, and what fpeech was't?

Ber. What did I fay *Poggio*?

Pog. Forfooth my Maifter faid, that hee loued her almoft afwell as hee loued Parmafent, and fwore (I'lebe fworne for him) that fhee wanted but fuch a Nofe as his was, to be as pretty a young woeman, as any was in *Parma*: *Do.* Oh grofe!

Ber. Nay Vnkle, then fhee ask't mee, whether my Father had any more children then my felfe: and I fayd no, 'twere better hee fhould haue had his braynes knockt out firft.

Do. This is intolerable.

Ber. Then fayd fhee, will *Signior Donado* your Vnkle leaue you all his wealth?

Do. Ha! that was good, did fhe harpe vpon that ftring?

Ber. Did fhe harpe vpon that ftring, I that fhe did: I anfwered, leaue me all his wealth? why woeman, hee hath no other wit, if hee had, he fhould heare on't to his euerlafting glory and confufion: I know (quoth I) I am his white boy, and will not be guld; and with that fhe fell into a great fmile, and went away. Nay I did fit her.

Do. Ah firrah, then I fee there is no changing of nature, Well *Bergetto*, I feare thou wilt be a very Affe ftill.

Ber. I fhould be forry for that Vnkle.

Do. Come, come you home with me, fince you are no better a fpeaker, I'le haue you wrixe to her after fome courtly manuer, and inclofe fome rich Iewell in the Letter.

Ber. I marry, that will be excellent.

Do. Peace Innocent,
Once in my time I'le fet my wits to fchoole,
If all faile, 'tis but the fortune of a foole.

Ber. *Poggio*, 'twill doe *Poggio*.   *Exeunt.*

C 3   *Actus*

Actus Secundus.

Enter Giouanni *and* Annabella, *as from their Chamber.*

Gio. Come *Annabella*, no more Sifter now,
But Loue; a name more Gracious, doe not blufh,
(Beauties fweete wonder) but be proud, to know
That yeelding thou haft conquer'd, and inflam'd
A heart whofe tribute is thy brothers life.

Anna. And mine is his, oh how thefe ftolne contents
Would print a modeft Crymfon on my cheekes,
Had any but my hearts delight preuail'd.

Gio. I maruaile why the chafter of your fex
Should thinke this pretty toye call'd *Maiden-head*,
So ftrange a loffe, when being loft, 'tis nothing,
And you are ftill the fame. *Anna.* 'Tis well for you,
Now you can talke. *Gio.* Muficke afwell confifts
In th'eare, as in the playing. *Anna.* Oh y'are wanton.
Tell on't, y'are beft, doe.

Gio. Thou wilt chide me then,
Kiffe me, fo; thus hung *Ioue* on *Leda's* necke,
And fuck't diuine *Ambrofia* from her lips:
I enuy not the mightieft man aliue,
But hold my felfe in being King of thee,
More great, then were I King of all the world:
But I fhall lofe you *Sweet-heart*.

Anna. But you fhall not. *Gio.* You muft be married Miftres.
Anna. Yes, to whom? *Gio.* Some one muft haue you.
Anna. You muft. *Gio.* Nay fome other.
Anna. Now, prithee do not fpeake fo, without iefting
You'le make me weepe in earneft.

Gio. What you will not.
But tell me fweete, can'ft thou be dar'd to fweare
That thou wilt liue to mee, and to no other?

Anna. By both our loues I dare, for didft thou know
My *Giouanni*, how all fuiters feeme
To my eyes hatefull, thou wouldft cruft mee then.

E3   *Gio.*

Gio. Enough, I take thy word; Sweet we must part,
Remember what thou vow'ft, keepe well my heart.

    Anna. Will you begon?   *Gio.* I muft.

    Anna. When to returne?   *Gio.* Soone.

    Anna. Looke you doe.   *Gio.* Farewell.   *Exit.*

    Anna. Goe where thou wilt, in mind I'le keepe thee here,
And where thou art, I know I fhall be there
Guardian.

              Enter Putana.

    Put. Child, how is't child? well, thanke Heauen, ha!

    Anna. O *Guardian*, what a Paradife of joy
Haue I paft ouer!

    Put. Nay what a Paradife of ioy haue you paft vnder?
why now I commend thee (*Chardge*) feare nothing, (fweete-
heart) what though hee be your Brother; your Brother's a
man I hope, and I fay ftill, if a young Wench feele the fitt vpon
her, let her take any body, Father or Brother, all is one.

    Anna. I would not haue it knowne for all the world.

    Put. Nor I indeed, for the fpeech of the people; elfe 'twere
Florio within---Daughter *Annabella.*   (nothing.

    Anna. O mee! my Father,--here Sir,— reach my worke.

    Flo. within. What are you doeing? *An.* So, let him come now,

    Enter Florio, Richardetto, *like a Doctor of Phificke,*
    and Philotis *with a Lute in her hand.*

    Flo. So hard at worke, that's well; you lofe no time', looke,
I haue brought you company, here's one, a learned Doctor, lately come from *Padua*, much skild in Phyficke, and for that I fee
you haue of late beene fickly, I entreated this reuerent man
to vifit you fome time.

    Anna. Y'are very welcome Sir.

    Fichard. I thanke you Miftreffe,
Loud Fame in large report hath fpoke your praife,
Afwell for Vertue as perfection:
For which I haue beene bold to bring with mee
A Kinf-woeman of mine, a maide, for fong,
And muficke, one perhaps will giue content,

                          Pleafe

pleafe you to know her,

Anna. They are parts I loue,
And fhee for them moft welcome.

Phi. Thanke you Lady,

Flo. Sir now you know my houfe, pray make not ftrange,
And if you finde my Daughter neede your Art,
I'le be your pay-mafter,

Rich. Sir, what I am fhee fhall command.

Flo. You fhall bind me to you,
Daughter, I muft haue conference with you,
About fome matters that concernes vs both.
Good Maifter Doctor, pleafe you but walke in,
Wee'le craue a little of your Cozens cunning :
I thinke my Girle hath not quite forgot
To touch an Inftrument, fhe could haue don't,
Wee'le heare them both.

Rich. I'le waite vpon you fir.　　　　*Exeunt.*
　　Enter Soranzo *in his ftudy reading a Booke.*
　Loues meafure is extreame, the comfort, paine :
　The life vnreft, and the reward difdaine
What's here? lookt o're againe, 'tis fo, fo writes
This fmooth licentious Poet in his rymes.
But *Sanazar* thou lyeft, for had thy bofome
Felt fuch oppreffion as is laid on mine,
Thou wouldft haue kift the rod that made the fmart.
To worke then happy Mufe, and contradict
What *Sanazar* hath in his enuy writ.
　Loues meafure is the meane, fweet his annoyes,
　His pleafures life, and his reward all ioyes.
Had *Annabella* liu'd when *Sanazar*
Did in his briefe *Enconium* celebrate
Venice that Queene of Citties, he had left
That Verfe which gaind him fuch a fume of Gold,
And for one onely looke from *Annabell*
Had writ of her, and her diuiner cheekes,
O how my thoughts are————
　Vafques within--Pray forbeare, in rules of Ciuility, let me giue
notice on't : I fhall be tax't of my neglect of duty and feruice.

　　　　　　　　　　　　　　　　　　　Soran.

Soran. What rude intrusion interrupts my peace,
Can I be no where priuate?

Vas. within. Troth you wrong your modesty.

Soran. What's the matter *Vasques*, who is't?

Enter Hippolita *and* Vasques.

Hip. 'Tis I:
Doe you know mee now? looke periurd man on her
Whom thou and thy distracted lust haue wrong'd,
Thy sensuall rage of blood hath made my youth
A scorne to men and Angels, and shall I
Be now a foyle to thy vnsated change?
Thou know'st (false wanton) when my modest fame
Stood free from staine, or scandall, all the charmes
Of Hell or sorcery could not preuaile
Against the honour of my chaster bosome.
Thyne eyes did pleade in teares, thy tongue in oathes
Such and so many, that a heart of steele
Would haue beene wrought to pitty, as was mine:
And shall the Conquest of my lawfull bed,
My husbands death vrg'd on by his disgrace,
My losse of woeman-hood be ill rewarded
With hatred and contempt? No, know *Soranzo*,
I haue a spirit doth as much distast
The slauery of fearing thee, as thou
Dost loath the memory of what hath past.

Soran. Nay deare *Hippolita.*

Hip. Call me not deare,
Nor thinke with supple words to smooth the grosenesse
Of my abuses; 'tis not your new Mistresse,
Your goodly *Madam Merchant* shall triumph
On my detection; tell her thus from mee,
My byrth was Nobler, and by much more Free.

Soran. You are too violent.

Hip. You are too double
In your dissimulation, see'st thou this,
This habit, these blacke mourning weedes of Care,
'Tis thou art cause of this, and hast diuorc't

D

My

My husband from his life and me from him,
And made me Widdow in my widdow-hood.

  Soran. Will you yet heare?

  Hip. More of the periuries?
Thy foule is drown'd too deepely in thofe finnes,
Thou need'ft not add to'th number.

  Soran. Then I'le leaue you,
You are paft all rules of fence.

  Hip. And thou of grace.

  Vaf. Fy Miftreffe, you are not neere the limits of reafon, if
my Lord had a refolution as noble as Vertue it felfe, you take the
courfe to vnedge it all. Sir I befeech you doe not perplexe her,
griefes (a'as) will haue a vent, I dare vndertake Madam *Hippo-*
lita will now freely heare you.

  Soran. Talke to a woman frantick, are thefe the fruits of your

  Hip. They are the fruites of thy vntruth, falfe man, (loue?
Didft thou not fweare, whil'ft yet my husband liu'd,
That thou wouldft wifh no happineffe on earth
More then to call me wife? didft thou not vow
When hee fhould dye to marry mee? for which
The Deuill in my blood, and thy protefts
Caus'd mee to Counfaile him to vndertake
A voyage to *Ligorne* , for that we heard,
His Brother there was dead, and left a Daughter
Young and vnfriended, who with much adoe
I wifh't him to bring hither ; hee did fo,
And went ; and as thou know'ft dyed on the way.
Vnhappy man to buy his death fo deare
With my aduice ; yet thou for whom I did it,
Forget'ft thy vowes, and leau'ft me to my fhame.

  Soran. Who could helpe this?

  Hip. Who? periur'd man thou couldft,
If thou hadft faith or loue.

  Soran. You are deceiu'd,
The vowes I made, (if you remember well)
Were wicked and vnlawfull, 'twere more finne
To keepe them, then to breake them ; as for mee

I cannot maske my penitence, thinke thou
How much thou haft digreft from honeft fhame,
In bringing of a gentleman to death
Who was thy husband, fuch a one as hee,
So noble in his quality, condition,
Learning, behauiour, entertainment, loue,
As *Parma* could not fhew a brauer man.

Vaf. You doe not well, this was not your promife.

Soran. I care not, let her know her monftrous life,
Ere I'le be feruile to fo blacke a finne,
I'le be a Curfe ; woeman, come here no more,
Learne to repent and dye ; for by my honour
I hate thee and thy luft ; you haue beene too foule.

Vaf. This part has beene fcuruily playd.

Hip. How foolifhly this beaft contemnes his Fate,
And fhuns the vfe of that, which I more fcorne
Then I once lou'd his loue ; but let him goe,
My vengeance fhall giue comfort to his woe.

She offers to goe away.

Vaf. Miftreffe, Miftreffe Madam *Hippolita,*
Pray a word or two.   *Hip.* With mee Sir ?

Vaf. With you if you pleafe.   *Hip.* What is't ?

Vaf. I know you are infinitely mou'd now , and you thinke
you haue caufe, fome I confeffe you haue, but fure not fo much
as you imagine.   *Hip.* Indeed.

Vaf. O you were miferably bitter, which you followed
euen to the laft fillable : Faith you were fomewhat too fhrewd,
by my life you could not haue tooke my Lord in a worfe time,
fince I firft knew him : to morrow you fhall finde him a new
man.   *Hip.* Well, I fhall waite his leafure.

Vaf. Fie, this is not a hearty patience, it comes fowerly from
you, troth let me perfwade you for once.

Hip. I haue it and it fhall be fo ; thanks opportunity
——— perfwade me to what ?———

Vaf. Vifitt him in fome milder temper , O if you could but
mafter a little your femall fpleen, how might you winne him !

Hip. Hee wil neuer loue me: *Vafques,* thou haft bin a too trufty
feruant to fuch a mafter, & I beleeue thy reward in the end wil fal

out like mine.   *Vas.* So perhaps too.

Hip. Resolue thy selfe it will; had I one so true, so truely ho-nest, so secret to my Counsels, as thou ha$\mathfrak{h}$ beene to him and his, I should thinke it a slight acquittance, not onely to make him Maister of all I haue, but euen of my selfe.

Vas. O you are a noble Gentlewoman.

Hip. Wu't thou feede alwayes vpon hopes? well, I know thou art wise, and see'st the reward of an old seruant daily what it is.   *Vas.* Beggery and neglect.

Hip. True, but *Vasques*, wer't thou mine, and wouldst bee priuate to me and my designes; I here protest my selfe, and all what I can else call myne, should be at thy dispose.

Vas. Worke you that way old moule? then I haue the wind of you —— I were not worthy of it, by any desert that could lye----within my compasse; if i could ——

Hip. What then?

Vas. I should then hope to liue in these my old yeares with rest and security.

Hip. Giue me thy hand, now promise but thy silence,
And helpe to bring to passe a plot I haue;
And here in sight of Heauen, (that being done)
I make thee Lord of mee and mine estate.

Vas. Come you are merry,
This is such a happinesse that I can
Neither thinke or beleeue.

Hip. Promise thy secresie, and 'tis confirm'd.

Vas. Then here I call our good *Genij* foe-witnesses, whatso-euer your designes are, or against whomsoeuer, I will not one-ly be a speciall actor therein, but neuer disclose it till it be effected.

Hip. I take thy word, and with that, thee for mine:
Come then, let's more conferre of this anon.
On this delicious bane my thoughts shall banquet,
Reuenge shall sweeten what my griefes haue tasted.   *Exeunt.*

Enter Richardetto *and* Philotis.

Richar. Thou see'st (my louely Neece) these strange mil-
How all my fortunes turne to my disgrace,   (haps,
Wherein I am but as a looker on,

Whiles

Whiles others act my shame, and I am silent.

Phi. But Vnkle, wherein can this borrowed shape
Giue you content?

Richard. I'le tell thee gentle Neece,
Thy wanton Aunt in her laciuious riotts
Liues now secure, thinkes I am surely dead
In my late Iourney to *Ligorne* for you ;
(As I haue caus'd it to be rumor'd out)
Now would I see with what an impudence
Shee giues scope to her loose adultery,
And how the Common voyce allowes hereof :
Thus farre I haue preuail'd.

Phi. Alas, I feare
You meane some strange reuenge.

Richard. O be not troubled,
Your ignorance shall pleade for you in all,
But to our businesse, what, you learnt for certaine
How *Signior Florio* meanes to giue his Daughter
In marriage to *Soranzo*?

Phi. Yes for certaine.

Richard. But how finde you young *Annabella's* loue,
Inclind to him ?

Phi. For ought I could perceiue,
Shee neyther fancies him or any else.

Richard. There's Mystery in that which time must shew,
Shee vs'd you kindly. *Phi.* Yes.

Richard. And crau'd your company ? *Phi.* Often.

Richard. 'Tis well, it goes as I could wish,
I am the Doctor now, and as for you,
None knowes you ; if all faile not we shall thriue.
But who comes here ? *Enter* Grimaldi.
I know him, 'tis *Grimaldi,*
A Roman and a souldier, neere allyed
Vnto the Duke of *Montferrato,* one
Attending on the *Nuntio* of the Pope
That now resides in *Parma,* by which meanes
He hopes to get the loue of *Annabella,*

Gri.

Gri. Saue you Sir.   *Richard.* And you Sir.

Gri. I haue heard
Of your approu'd skill, which through the City
Is freely talkt of, and would craue your ayd.

Richard. For what Sir?

Gri. Marry sir for this——
But I would speake in Priuate.

Richard. Leaue vs Cozen.   *Exit Phi:*

Gri. I loue faire *Annabella*, and would know
Whether in Arts there may not be receipts
To moue affection.

Richard. Sir perhaps there may;
But these will nothing profit you.

Gri. Not mee?

Richard. Vnlesse I be mistooke, you are a man
Greatly in fauour with the Cardinall.

Gri. What of that?

Richard. In duty to his Grace,
I will be bold to tell you, if you seeke
To marry *Florio's* daughter, you must first
Remoue a barre twixt you and her.

Gri. Whose that?

Richard. *Soranzo* is the man that hath her heart,
And while hee liues, be sure you cannot speed.

Gri. Soranzo, what mine Enemy, is't hee?

Richard. Is hee your Enemy?

Gri. The man I hate,
Worse then Confusion;
I'le tell him streight.

Richard. Nay, then take mine aduice,
(Euen for his Graces sake the Cardinall)
I'le finde a time when hee and shee doe meete,
Of which I'le giue you notice, and to be sure
Hee shall not scape you, I'le prouide a poyson
To dip your Rapiers poynt in, if hee had
As many heads as *Hidra* had, he dyes.

Gri. But shall I trust thee Doctor?

E 2   *Richard.*

Richard. As your ſelfe,
Doubt not in ought; thus ſhall the Fates decree,
By me *Soranzo* falls, that min'd mee.　　　*Exeunt.*
　　　Enter Donado, Bergetto *and* Poggio.

Do. Well Sir, I muſt bee content to be both your Secretary
and your Meſſenger my ſelfe; I cannot tell what this Letter may
worke, but as ſure as I am aliue, if thou come once to talke with
her, I feare thou wu't marre whatſoeuer I make.

Ben. You make Vnkle? why am not I bigge enough to carry mine owne Letter I pray?

Do. I, I carry a fooles head o'thy owne; why thou Dunce,
wouldſt thou write a letter, and carry it thy ſelfe?

Ber. Yes that I wudd, and reade it to her with my owne
mouth; for you muſt thinke, if ſhee will not beleeue me my ſelfe
when ſhe heares me ſpeake; ſhe will not beleeue anothers hand-
writing. O you thinke I am a blocke-head Vnkle, no ſir, *Pog-*
gio knowes I haue indited a letter my ſelfe, ſo I haue.

Pog. Yes truely ſir, I haue it in my pocket.

Do. A ſweete one no doubt, pray let's ſee't.

Ber. I cannot reade my owne hand very well *Poggio,*
Reade it *Poggio.*

Do. Begin.

　　　　　Poggio reades.

Pog. MOſt dainty and honey-ſweete Miſtreſſe, I could call
you faire, and lie as faſt as any that loues you, but
my Vnkle being the elder man, I leaue it to him, as more fit for
his age, and the colour of his beard; I am wiſe enough to tell you
I can board where I ſee occaſion, or if you like my Vnkles wit better then mine, you ſhall marry mee; if you like mine better then
his, I will marry you in ſpight of your teeth; So commending my
beſt parts to you, I reſt.　　Yours vpwards and downewards,
　　　　　or you may choſe,　　*Bergetto.*

Ber. Ah ha, here's ſtuffe Vnkle.

Do. Here's ſtuffe indeed to ſhame vs all,
Pray whoſe aduice did you take in this learned Letter?

Pog. None vpon my word, but mine owne.

　　　　　　　　　　　　　　　　　　　　Ber.

Ber. And mine Vnkle, beleeue it, no bodies elfe ; 'twas mine owne brayne, I thanke a good wit for't.

Do. Get you home fir , and looke yon keepe within doores till I returne.

Ber. How ? that were a ieft indeede ; I fcorne it yfaith.

Do. What you doe not ?

Ber. Iudge me, but I doe now.

Pog. Indeede fir 'tis very vnhealthy.

Do. Well fir, if I heare any of your apifh running to motions, and fopperies till I come backe , you were as good no ; looke too't.   *Exit Do.*

Ber. Poggio, fhall's fteale to fee this Horfe with the head in's

Pog. I but you muft take heede of whipping.   (tayle?

Ber. Doft take me for a Child *Poggio*,

Come honeft *Poggio*.   *Exeunt.*

Enter Fryar *and* Giouanni.

Fry. Peace, thou haft told a tale, whofe euery word
Threatens eternall flaughter to the foule :
I'me forry I haue heard it ; would mine eares
Had beene one minute deafe, before the houre
That thou cam'ft to mee : *O young man* caft-away,
By the relligious number of mine order,
I day and night haue wak't my aged eyes,
Aboue thy ftrength, to weepe on thy behalfe :
But Heauen is angry, and be thou refolu'd,
Thou art a man remark't to taft a mifchiefe,
Looke for't ; though it come late, it will come fure.

Gio. Father, in this you are vncharitable ;
What I haue done, I'le proue both fit and good.
It is a principall (which you haue taught
When I was yet your Scholler) that the Fame
And Compofition of the *Minde* doth follow
The Frame and Compofition of *Body* :
So where the *Bodies* furniture is *Beauty*,
The *Mindes* muft needs be *Vertue* : which allowed,
Vertue it felfe is *Reafon but refin'd*,
And *Loue* the Quintefence of that, this proues

My

My Sifters *Beauty* being rarely *Faire,*
Is rarely *Vertuous* ; chiefely in her loue,
And chiefely in that *Loue,* her loue to me.
If *hers to me,* then fo is *mine to her* ;
Since in like Caufes are effects alike.

   Fry. O ignorance in knowledge, long agoe,
How often haue I warn'd thee this before?
Indeede if we were fure there were no *Deity,*
Nor *Heauen* nor *Hell,* then to be lead alone,
By Natures light (as were Philofophers
Of elder times) might inftance fome defence.
But 'tis not fo ; then Madman, thou wilt finde,
That *Nature* is in Heauens pofitions blind.

   Gio. Your age o're rules you , had you youth like mine,
You'd make her loue your heauen, and her diuine.

   Fry. Nay then I fee th'art too farre fold to hell,
It lies not in the Compaffe of my prayers
To call thee backe ; yet let me Counfell thee :
Perfwade thy fifter to fome marriage.

   Gio. Marriage? why that's to dambe her ; that's to proue
Her greedy of variety of luft.

   Fry. O fearefull! if thou wilt not, giue me leaue
To fhriue her ; left fhee fhould dye vn-abfolu'd.

   Gio. At your beft leafure Father, then fhee'le tell you,
How dearely fhee doth prize my Matchleffe loue,
Then you will know what pitty 'twere we two
Should haue beene fundred from each others armes,
View well her face, and in that little round,
You may obferue a world of variety ;
For Colour, lips, for fweet perfumes, her breath ;
For Iewels, eyes ; for threds of pureft gold,
Hayre ; for delicious choyce of Flowers, cheekes ;
Wonder in euery portion of that Throne :
Heare her but fpeake, and you will fweare the Sphæres
Make Muficke to the Cittizens in Heauen :
But Father, what is elfe for pleafure fram'd,
Leaft I offend your eares fhall goe vn-nam'd.

Fry. The more I heare, I pitty thee the more,
That one so excellent should giue those parts
All to a second Death; what I can doe
Is but to pray; and yet I could aduise thee,
Wouldst thou be rul'd.

Gio. In what?

Fry. Why leaue her yet,
The Throne of *Mercy* is aboue your trespasse,
Yet time is left you both----

Gio. To embrace each other,
Else let all time be strucke quite out of number;
Shee is like mee, and I like her resolu'd.

Fry. No more, I'le visit her; this grieues me most,
Things being thus, a paire of soules are lost. *Exeut.*

Enter Florio, Donado, Annabella, Putana.

Flo. Where's *Giouanni*?

Anna. Newly walk't abroad,
And (as I heard him say) gon to the Fryar
His reuerent Tutor.

Flo. That's a blessed man,
A man made vp of holinesse, I hope
Hee'le teach him how to gaine another world.

Do. Faire Gentlewoman, here's a letter sent
To you from my young Cozen, I dare sweare
He loues you in his soule, would you could heare
Sometimes, what I see dayly, sighes and teares,
As if his breast were prison to his heart.

Flo. Receiue it *Annabella*.

Anna. Alas good man.

Do. What's that she said?

Pu. And please you sir, she sayd, alas good man, truely I doe
Commend him to her euery night before her first sleepe, because
I wou'd haue her dreame of him, and shee harkens to that most
relligiously.

Do. Say'st so, godamercy *Putana*, there's something for thee,
and prythee doe what thou canst on his behalfe; sha'not

be

be lost labour, take my word for't.

Pu. Thanke you most heartily sir, now I haue a *Feeling* of your mind, let mee alone to worke.

Anna. Guardian!

Pu. Did you call?

Anna. Keepe this letter,
Do. Signior Florio, in any case bid her reade it instantly.

Flo. Keepe it for what? pray reade it mee here right.

Anna. I shall sir,   *She reades.*

Do. How d'ee finde her inclin'd *Signior?*

Flo. Troth sir I know not how; not all so well
As I could wish.

Anna. Sir I am bound to rest your Cozens debter,
The Iewell I'le returne; for if he loue,
I'le count that loue a Iewell.

Do. Marke you that?
Nay keepe them both sweete Maide.

Anna. You must excuse mee,
Indeed I will not keepe it.

Flo. Where's the Ring,
That which your Mother in her will bequeath'd,
And charg'd you on her blessing not to giue't
To any but your Husband? send backe that.

Anna. I haue it not.

Flo. Ha! haue it not, where is't?

Anna. My brother in the morning tooke it fró me,
Said he would weare't to Day.

Flo. Well, what doe you say
To young *Bergetto's* loue? are you content
To match with him? speake.

Do. There's the poynt indeed.

Anna. What shal I doe, I must say something now.

Flo. What say, why d'ee not speake?

Anna. Sir with your leaue.
Please you to giue me freedome.

Flo. Yes you haue.

Anna. Signior *Donado,* if your Nephew meane

                        To

To rayse his better Fortunes in his match,
The hope of mee will hinder such a hope;
Sir if you loue him, as I know you doe;
Find one more worthy of his choyce then mee;
In short, I'me sure, I sha'not be his wife.

   Do. Why here's plaine dealing, I commend thee for't,
And all the worst I wish thee, is heauen blesse thee,
Your Father yet and I will still be friends,
Shall we not *Signior Florio* ?

   Flo. Yes, why not?
Looke here your Cozen comes.

      Enter Bergetto *and* Poggio.

   Do. Oh Coxcombe, what doth he make here?

   Ber. Where's my Vnkle sirs.

   Do. What's the newes now?

   Ber. Saue you Vnkle, saue you, you must not thinke I come
for nothing Maisters, and how and how is't? what you haue
read my letter, ah, there I---- tickled you yfaith.

   Pog. But 'twere better you had tickled her in another place.

   Ber. Sirrah *Sweet-heart*, I'le tell thee a good jest, and riddle
what 'tis.

   Anna. You say you'd tell mee.

   Ber. As I was walking iust now in the Streete, I mett a
swaggering fellow would needs take the wall of me, and because hee did thrust me, I very valiantly cal'd him *Rogue*, hee
hereupon bad me drawe; I told him I had more wit then so, but
when hee saw that I would not, hee did so maule me with the
hilts of his Rapier, that my head sung whil'st my feete caper'd
in the kennell.

   Do. Was euer the like asse seene?

   Anna. And what did you all this while?

   Ber. Laugh at him for a gull, till I see the blood runne about
mine eares, and then I could not choose but finde in my
heart to cry; till a fellow with a broad beard, (they say hee
is a new-come Doctor) cald mee into this house, and gaue me a
playster, looke you here 'tis; and sir there was a young wench
washt my face and hands most excellently, yfaith I shall loue
                        her

her as long as I liue for't, did she not *Poggio* ?

Pog. Yes and kist him too.

Ber. Why la now, you thinke I tell a lye Vnkle I warrant.

Do. Would hee that beate thy blood ont of thy head, had beaten some wit into it; For I feare thou neuer wilt haue any.

Ber. Oh Vnkle, but there was a wench, would haue done a mans heart good to haue lookt on her, by this light, shee had a face mee-thinks worth twenty of you Mistresse *Annabella.*

Do. Was euer such a foole borne?

Anna. I am glad shee lik't you sir.

Ber. Are you so, by my troth I thanke you forsooth.

Flo. Sure 'twas the Doctors neece, that was last day with vs here.

Ber. 'Twas shee, 'twas shee.

Do. How doe you know that simplicity ?

Ber. Why doe's not hee say so? if I should haue sayd no, I should haue giuen him the lye *Vnkle*, and so haue deseru'd a dry beating againe ; I'le none of that.

Flo. A very modest welbehau'd young Maide as I haue seene.

Do. Is shee indeed ?

Flo. Indeed
Shee is, if I haue any Iudgement.

Do. Well sir, now you are free, you need not care for sending letters, now you are dismist, your Mistresse here will none of you.

Ber. No; why what care I for that, I can haue Wenches enough in *Parma* for halfe a Crowne a peece, cannot I *Poggio*?

Pog. I'le warrant you sir.

Do. Signior Florio, I thanke you for your free recourse you gaue for my admittance ; and to you faire Maide that Iewell I will giue you 'gainst your marriage, come will you goe sir ?

Ber. I marry will I Mistres, farwell Mistres, I'le come againe to morrow---farwell Mistres. *Exit Do. Ber, & Pog.*

Enter Gio.

Flo. Sonne, where haue you beene? what alone, alone, still, still? I would not haue it so, you must forsake this ouer bookish humour. Well, your Sister hath shooke the Foole off.

Gio.

Gio. 'Twas no match for her.

Flo. 'Twas not indeed I ment it nothing lesse,
Soranzo is the man I onely like;
Looke on him *Annabella*, come, 'tis supper-time,
And it growes late.　　　　　　　*Exit* Florio.

Gio. Whose Iewell's that?

Anna. Some Sweet-hearts.

Gio. So I thinke.

Anna. A lusty youth, *Signior Donado* gaue it me
To weare againlt my Marriage.

Gio. But you shall not weare it, send it him backe againe.

Anna. What, you are jealous?

Gio. That you shall know anon, at better leasure:
Welcome sweete night, the Euening crownes the Day. *Exeunt.*

Actus Tertius.

Enter Bergetto *and* Poggio.

Ber. DO'es my Vnkle thinke to make mee a Baby still? no,
　　　　Poggio, he shall know, I hauea skonce now.

Pog. I let him not bobbe you off like an Ape with an apple.

Ber. Sfoot, I will haue the wench, if he were tenne Vnkles,
in delpight of his nose *Poggio*.　　　　　　　　　　　　(ground,

Pog. Hold him to the Grynd-stone, and giue not a jot of
Shee hath in a manner promised you already.

Pog. True *Poggio*, and her Vnkle the Doctor
Swore I should marry her.

Pog. He swore I remember.

Ber. And I will haue her that's more; did'st see the codpeice-
poynt she gaue me, and the box of Mermalade?

Pog. Very well, and kist you, that my chopps watred at the
fight on't; there's no way but to clap vp a marriage in hugger
mugger.

Ber. I will do't for I tell thee *Poggio*, I begin to grow valiant
　　　　　　　　　　　　　　　　　　　　　　　methinks,

methinkes, and my courage begins to riſe.

Pog. Should you be afraid of your Vnkle?

Ber. Hang him old doating Raſcall, no, I ſay I will haue her.

Pog. Loſe no time then.

Ber. I will beget a race of Wiſe men and Conſtables, that ſhall cart whoores at their owne charges, and breake the Dukes peace ere I haue done my ſelfe.——— come away.   ～ *Exeunt.*

     Enter Florio, Giouanni, Soranzo, Annabella,
           Putana *and* Vaſques.

  Flo. My Lord *Soranzo*, though I muſt confeſſe,
The proffers that are made me, haue beene great
In marriage of my daughter ; yet the hope
Of your ſtill riſing honours, haue preuaild
Aboue all other Ioynctures ; here ſhee is,
She knowes my minde, ſ eake for your ſelfe to her,
And heare you daughter, ſee you vſe him nobly,
For any priuat e ſpeech, I'le giue you time :
Come ſonne and you, the reſt let them alone,
Agree as they may.

  Soran. I thanke you ſir.

  Gio. Siſter be not all wooman, thinke on me.

  Soran. Vaſques?   *Vaſ.* My Lord.

  Soran. Attend me without——— *Exeunt omnes, manet* Soran.

  Anna. Sir what's your will with me?   (*& Anna.*

  Soran. Doe you not know what I ſhould tell you ?

  Anna. Yes, you'le ſay you loue mee.

  Soran. And I'le ſweare it too ; will you beleeue it ?

  Anna. 'Tis not poynt of faith.

       Enter Giouanni *aboue.*

  Soran. Haue you not will to loue?

  Anna. Not you.   *Soran.* Whom then ?

  Anna. That's as the Fates inferre.

  Gio. Of thoſe I'me regient now.

  Soran. What meane you ſweete?

  Anna. To liue and dye a Maide.

                               Soran.

Soran. Ch that's vnfit.

Gio. Here's one can say that's but a womans noate.

Soran. Did you but see my heart, then would you sweare——

Anna. That you were dead.

Gio. That's true, or somewhat neere it.

Soran. See you these true loues teares?

Anna. No.   *Gio.* Now shee winkes.

Soran. They plead to you for grace.

Anna. Yet nothing speake.

Soran. Oh grant my suite.

Anna. What is't   *Soran.* To let mee liue.

Anna. Take it——

Soran. Still yours.——

Anna. That is not mine to giue.

Gio. One such another word would kil his hopes.

Soran. Mistres, to leaue those fruitlesse strifes of wit,
I know I haue lou'd you long, and lou'd you truely;
Not hope of what you haue, but what you are
Haue drawne me on, then let mee not in vaine
Still feele the rigour of your chast disdaine.
I'me sicke, and sicke to th'heart.

Anna. Helpe, *Aquavitæ.*

Soran. What meane you?

Anna. Why I thought you had beene sicke.

Soran. Doe you mocke my loue?

Gio. There sir shee was too nimble.

Soran. 'Tis plaine; shee laughes at me, these scornefull taunts
neither become your modesty, or yeares.

Anna. You are no looking-glasse, or if you were, I'de dresse
my language by you.

Gio. I'me confirm'd——

Anna. To put you out of doubt, my Lord, mee-thinks your
Common sence should make you vnderstand, that if I lou'd you,
or desir'd your loue, some way I should haue giuen you better
tast: but since you are a Noble man, and one I wouldnot wish
should spend his youth in hopes, let mee aduise you here, to forbeare your suite, and thinke I wish you well, I tell you this.

Soran.

Soran. Is't you speake this?

Anna. Yes, I my selfe; yet know.
Thus farre I giue you comfort, if mine eyes
Could haue pickt out a man (among'st all those
That sue'd to mee) to make a husband of,
You should haue beene that man; let this suffice,
Be noble in your secresie and wise.

   Gio. Why now I see shee loues me.

   Anna. One word more:
As euer Vertue liu'd within your mind,
As euer noble courses were your guide,
As euer you would haue me know you lou'd me,
Let not my Father know hereof by you:
If I hereafter finde that I must marry,
It shall be you or none.

   Soran. I take that promise.

   Anna. Oh, oh my head.

   Soran. What's the matter, not well?

   Anna. Oh I begin to sicken.

   Gio. Heauen forbid.   *Exit from aboue.*

   Soran. Helpe, helpe, within there ho:

   Gio. Looke to your daughter *Signior Florio.*

Enter Florio, Gionanni, Putana.

   Flo. Hold her vp, shee sounes.

   Gio. Sister how d'ee?

   Anna. Sicke, brother, are you there?

   Flo. Conuay her to her bed instantly, whil'st I send for a Phisitian, quickly I say.

   Put. Alas poore Child.   *Exeunt, manet* Soranzo.

Enter Vasques.

   Vas. My Lord.

   Soran. Oh *Vasques*, now I doubly am vndone,
Both in my present and my future hopes:
Shee plainely told me, that shee could not loue,
And thereupon soone sickned, and I feare
Her life's in danger.

                   F

                                   Vas.

Vaf. Byr lady Sir, and fo is yours, if you knew all.——'las fir,
I am forry for that, may bee 'tis but the *Maides ficknesse*, an o-
uer-fluxe of youth, and then fir, there is no fuch prefent remedy,
as prefent Marriage. But hath fhee giuen you an abfolute
deniall ?

Soran. She hath and fhe hath not; I'me full of griefe,
But what fhe fayd, I'le tell thee as we goe. *Exeunt.*

Enter Giouanni *and* Putana.

Put. Oh fir, wee are all vndone, quite vndone, vtterly vndone,
And fham'd foreuer ; your fifter, oh your fifter.

Gio. What of her ? for Heauens fake fpeake, how do'es fhee?

Put. Oh that euer I was borne to fee this day.

Gio. She is not dead, ha, is fhee ?

Put. Dead ? no, fhee is quicke, 'tis worfe, fhe is with childe,
You know what you haue done ; Heauen forgiue 'ee,
'Tis too late to repent, now Heauen helpe vs.

Gio. With child ? how doft thou know't ?

Put. How doe I know't? am I at thefe yeeres ignorant, what
the meaning's of Quames, and Waterpangs be ? of changing of
Colours, Quezineffe of ftomacks, Pukings, and another thing
that I could name; doe not (for her and your Credits fake) fpend
the time in asking how, and which way, 'tis fo ; fhee is quick
vpon my word, if you let a Phifitian fee her water y'are
vndone.

Gio. But in what cafe is fhee ?

Put. Prettily amended, 'twas but a fit which I foone efpi'd,
and fhe muft looke for often hence-forward.

Gio. Commend me to her, bid her take no care,
Let not the Doctor vifit her I chaige you,
Make fome excufe, till I returne; *oh mee,*
I haue a world of bufineffe in my head,
Doe not difcomfort her ; how doe this newes perplex mee !
If my Father come to her, tell him fhee's recouer'd well,
Say 'twas but fome ill dyet ; d'ee heare *Woeman,*
Looke you to't.

Put. I will fir. *Exeunt.*
Enter

Enter Florio *and* Richardetto

Flo. And how d'ee finde her sir?

Richard. Indifferent well,
I see no danger, scarse perceiue shee's sicke,
But that shee told mee, shee had lately eaten
Mellownes, and as shee thought, those disagreed
With her young stomacke.

Flo. Did you giue her ought?

Richard. An easie surfeit water, nothing else,
You neede not doubt her health; I rather thinke
Her sicknesse is a fulnesse of her blood,
You vnderstand mee?

Flo. I doe; you counsell well,
And once within these few dayes, will so order't
She shall be married, ere shee know the time.

Richard. Yet let not hast(sir)make vnworthy choice,
That were dishonour.

Flo. Maister Doctor no,
I will not doe so neither; in plaine words
My Lord *Soranzo* is the man I meane.

Richard. A noble and a vertuous Gentleman,

Flo. As any is in *Parma*; not farre hence,
Dwels Father *Bonauenture*, a graue Fryar,
Once Tutor to my Sonne; now at his Cell
I'le haue 'em married.

Richard. You haue plotted wisely.

Flo. I'le send one straight
To speake with him to night.

Richard. *Soranzo's* wife, he will delay no time:

Flo. It shall be so.

Enter Fryar *and* Giouanni.

Fry. Good peace be here and loue.

Flo. Welcome relligious Fryar, you are one,
That still bring blessing to the place you come to.

Gio. Sir, with what speed I could, I did my best,
To draw this holy man from forth his Cell,
To visit my sicke sister, that with words

Of ghostly comfort in this time of neede,
Hee might absolue her, whether she liue or dye.

Flo. 'Twas well done *Giouanni*, thou herein
Hast shewed a Christians care, a Brothers loue
Come Father, I'le conduct you to her chamber.
And one thing would intreat you.

Fry. Say on sir.

Flo. I haue a Fathers deare impression,
And wish before I fall into my graue,
That I might see her married, as 'tis fit;
A word from you *Graue man*, will winne her more,
Then all our best perswasions.

Fry. Gentle Sir,
All this I'le say, that Heauen may prosper her.   *Exeunt.*

Enter Grimaldi.

Gri. Now if the Doctor keepe his word, *Soranzo*,
Twenty to one you misse your Bride; I know
'Tis an vnnoble act, and not becomes
A Souldiers vallour; but in termes of loue,
Where Merite cannot sway, Policy must.
I am resolu'd, if this Phisitian
Play not on both hands, then *Soranzo* falls.

Enter Richardetto.

Richa'd. You are come as I could wish, this very night Soranzo, 'tis ordain'd must bee affied to *Annabella*; and for ought
I know, married.   *Gri.* How I

Richard. Yet your patience,
The place, 'tis Fryars *Bonauentures* Cell.
Now I would wish you to bestow this night,
In watching thereabouts, 'tis but a night,
If you misse now, to morrow I'le know all.

Gri. Haue you the poyson?

Richard. Here 'tis in this Box,
Doubt nothing, this will doe't; in any case
As you respect your life, be quicke and sure.

Gri. I'le speede him.

Richard. Doe; away, for 'tis not safe

You

You ſhould be ſeene much here — euer my loue.

  Gri. And mine to you.   *Exit* Gri.

  Richard. So, if this hitt, I'le laugh and hug reuenge ;
And they that now dreame of a wedding-feaſt,
May chance to mourne the luſty Bridegromes ruine.
But to my other buſineſſe ; Neice *Philotis.*

          Enter Philotis.

  Phi. Vnkle.

  Richard. My louely Neece, you haue bethought 'ee.

  Phi. Yes, and as you counſel'd,
Faſhion'd my heart to loue him, but hee ſweares
Hee will to night be married ; for he feares
His Vnkle elſe, if hee ſhould know the drift,
Will hinder all, and call his Couze to ſhrift.

  Richard. To night? why beſt of all ; but let mee ſee,
I ha —— yes, —— ſo it ſhall be ; in diſguiſe
Wee'le earely to the Fryars, I haue thought on't.

       Enter Bergetto *and* Poggio.

  Phi. Vnkle, hee comes.

  Richard. Welcome my worthy Couze.

  Ber. I aſſe pretty Laſſe, come buſſe Laſſe, a ha *Poggio.*

  Phi. There's hope of this yet.

  Richard. You ſhall haue time enough, withdraw a litt'e,
Wee muſt conferre at large.

  Ber. Haue you not ſweete-meates, or dainty deuices for me ?

  Phi. You ſhall enough *Sweet-heart.*

  Ber. Sweet-heart, marke that *Poggio* ; by my troth I cannot
chooſe but kiſſe thee once more for that word *Sweet-heart* ; *Poggio*, I haue a monſtrous ſwelling about my ſtomacke, whatſoeuer
the matter be.

  Pog. You ſhall haue Phiſick for't ſir.

  Richard. Time runs apace.

  Ber. Time's a blockhead.

  Richard. Be ru'd, when wee haue done what's fitt to doe,
Then you may kiſſe your fill, and bed her too.   *Exeunt.*

Enter the Fryar in his study, sitting in a chayre, Annabella *knee-ling and whispering to him, a Table before them and wax-lights, she weepes, and wrings her hands.*

Fry. I am glad to fee this pennance ; for beleeue me,
You haue vnript a foule, fo foule and guilty.
As I muft tell you true, I maruaile how
The earth hath borne you vp, but weepe, weepe on,
Thefe teares may doe you good ; weepe fafter yet,
Whiles I doe reade a Lecture.

Anna. Wretched creature.

Fry. I, you are wretched, miferably wretched,
Almoft condemn'd aliue ; there is *a place*
(Lift daughter) in a blacke and hollow Vault,
Where day is neuer feene ; there fhines no Sunne,
But flaming horrour of confuming Fires ;
A lightleffe Suphure, choakt with fmoaky foggs
Of an infected darkneffe ; in *this place*
Dwell many thoufand, thoufand fundry forts
Of neuer dying deaths ; there damned foules
Roare without pitty, there are Gluttons fedd
With Toades and Addars ; there is burning Oyle
Powr'd downe the Drunkards throate, the Vfurer
Is fore't to fupp whole draughts of molten Gold;
There is the Murtherer for-euer ftab'd,
Yet can he neuer dye ; there lies the wanton
On Racks of burning fteele, whiles in his foule
Hee feeles the torment of his raging luft.

Anna. Mercy, oh mercy.

Fry There ftands thefe wretched things,
Who haue dream't out whole yeeres in lawleffe fheets
And fecret incefts, curfing one another ;
Then you will wifh, each kiffe your brother gaue,
Had beene a Daggers poynt ; then you fhall heare
How hee will cry, oh would my wicked fifter
Had firft beene damn'd, when fhee did yeeld to luft.

But

But soft, methinkes I see repentance worke
New motions in your heart, say? how is't with you?

Anna. Is there no way left to redeeme my miseries?

Fry. There is, despaire not; Heauen is mercifull,
And offers grace euen now; 'tis thus agreed,
First, for your Honours safety that you marry
The Lord *Soranzo*, next, to saue your soule,
Leaue off this life, and henceforth liue to him.

Anna. Ay mee.

Fry. Sigh not, I know the baytes of sinne
Are hard to leaue, oh 'tis a death to doe't.
Remember what must come, are you content?

Anna. I am.

Fry. I like it well, wee'le take the time,
Who's neere vs there?

        Enter Florio, Giouanni.

Flo. Did you call Father?

Fry. Is Lord *Soranzo* come?

Flo. Hee stayes belowe.

Fry. Haue you acquainted him at full?

Flo. I haue and hee is ouer-ioy'd.

Fry. And so are wee: bid him come neere.

Gio. My Sister weeping, ha? I feare this *Fryars* falshood,
I will call him.   *Exit.*

Flo. Daughter, are you resolu'd?

Anna. Father, I am.

      Enter Giouanni, Soranzo, *and* Vasques.

Flo. My Lord *Soranzo*, here
Giue mee your hand, for that I giue you this.

Soran. Lady, say you so too?

Anna. I doe, and vow, to liue with you and yours.

Fry. Timely resolu'd:
My blessing rest on both, more to be done,
You may performe it on the Morning-sun.   *Exeunt.*

                              Enter

Enter Grimaldi *with his Rapier drawne,
and a Darke-lanthorne.*

Gri. 'Tis early night as yet, and yet too soone
To finish such a worke; here I will lye
To listen who comes next.   *Hee lies downe.*

Enter Bergetto *and* Philotis *disguis'd, and after*
Richardetto *and* Poggio.

Ber. Wee are almost at the place, I hope *Sweet-heart.*

Gri. I heare them neere, and heard one say *Sweet-heart,*
'Tis hee; now guide my hand some angry *Iustice*
Home to his bosome, now haue at you sir.   *strikes* Ber. *& Exit.*

Ber. Oh helpe, helpe, here's a stich fallen in my gutts,
Oh for a Flesh-taylor quickly —— *Poggio.*

Phi. What ayles my loue?

Ber. I am sure I cannot pisse forward and backward, and yet
I am wet before and behind, lights, lights, ho lights.

Phi. Alas, some Villaine here has slaine my loue.

Richard. Oh Heauen forbid it; raise vp the next neighbours
Instantly *Poggio,* and bring lights,   *Exit* Poggio.
How is't *Bergetto*? slaine?
It cannot be; are you sure y'are hurt?

Ber. O my belly seeths like a Porridge-pot, some cold water
I shall boyle ouer else; my whole body is in a sweat, that you
may wring my shirt; feele here—— why *Poggio.*

Enter Poggio *with Officers, and lights and Halberts.*

Pog. Here; alas, how doe you?

Richard. Giue me a light; what's here? all blood! O sirs,
Signior Donado's Nephew now is slaine,
Follow the murtherer with all the haste
Vp to the Citty, hee cannot be farre hence,
Follow I beseech you.

Officers. Follow, follow, follow.   *Exeunt Officers.*
                                                          Richard.

Richard. Teare off thy linnen Couz, to stop his wounds,
Be of good comfort man.

Ber. Is all this mine owne b'ood? nay then good-night with
me, *Poggio*, commend me to my Vnkle, dost heare? bid him for
my sake make much of this wench, oh---I am going the wrong
way sure, my belly akes so——oh farwell, *Poggio*---oh---
oh----   *Dyes.*

Phi. O hee is dead.

Pog. How ! dead !

Richard. Hee's dead indeed,
'Tis now to late to weepe, let's haue him home,
And with what speed we may, finde out the Murtherer.

Pog. Oh my Maister, my Maister, my Maister.   *Exeunt.*

Enter Vasques *and* Hippolita.

Hip. Betroath'd ?

Vas. I saw it.

Hip. And when's the marriage-day ?

Vas. Some two dayes hence.

Hip. Two dayes ? Why man I would but wish two houres
To send him to his last, and lasting sleepe.
And *Vasques* thou shalt see, I'le doe it brauely.

Vas. I doe not doubt your wisedome, nor (I trust) you my
I am infinitely yours.   (secresie,

Hip. I wilbe thine in spight of my disgrace,
So soone ? o wicked man, I durst be sworne,
Hee'd laugh to see mee weepe.

Vas. And that's a Villanous fault in him.

Hip. No, let him laugh, I'me arm'd in my resolues,
Be thou still true.

Vas. I should get little by treachery against so hopefull a preferment, as I am like to climbe to.

Hip. Euen to my bosome *Vasques*, let *My youth*
Reuell in these new pleasures, if wee thriue,
Hee now hath but a paire of dayes to liue.   *Exeunt.*

Enter Florio, Donado, Richardetto, Poggio *and Officers.*

Flo. 'Tis bootlesse now to shew your selfe a child

Signior Donado, what is done, is done ;
Spend not the time in teares, but seeke for Iustice.

Richard. I must confesse somewhat I was in fault,
That had not first acquainted you what loue
Past twixt him and my Neece; but as I liue,
His Fortune grieues me as it were mine owne.

Do. Ala. poore Creature, he ment no man harme,
That I am sure of.

Flo. I beleeue that too;
But stay my Maisters, are you sure you saw
The Murtherer passe here ?

Offic. And it pleafe you sir, wee are sure wee saw a Ruffian
with a naked weapon in his hand all bloody, get into my Lord
Cardinals Graces gate, that wee are sure of ; but for feare of his
Grace (blesse vs) we durst goe no further.

Do. Know you what manner of man hee was ?

Offic. Yes sure I know the man, they say a is a fouldier, hee
that lou'd your daughter Sir an't pleafe y'ee, 'twas hee for certaine.

Flo. *Grimaldi* oh my life.

Offic. I, I, the same.

Richard. The Cardinall is Noble, he no doubt
Will giue true Iustice.

Do. Knocke some one at the gate,

Pog. I'le knocke sir.   *Poggio knocks.*

Seruant within. What would 'ee ?

Flo. Wee require speech with the Lord Cardinall
About some present busineffe, pray informe
His Grace, that we are here.

Enter Cardinall and Grimaldi

Car. Why how now friends? what sawcy mates are
That know nor duty nor Ciuillity?   (you
Are we a person fit to be your hoast ?
Or is our house become your common Inne
To beate our dores at pleasure ? what such haste
Is yours as that it cannot waite fit times ?

                                                    Are

Are you the Maisters of this Common-wealth,
And know no more discretion? oh your newes
Is here before you, you haue lost a Nephew
Donado, last night by *Grimaldi* slaine:
Is that your businesse? well sir, we haue knowledge on't.
Le that suffice.

 Gri. In presence of your Grace,
In thought I neuer ment *Bergetto* harme,
But *Florio* you can tell, with how much scorne
Soranzo backt with his Confederates,
Hath often wrong'd mee; I to be reueng'd,
(For that I could not win him else to fight)
Had thought by way of Ambush to haue kild him,
But was vnluckely, therein mistooke;
Else hee had felt what late *Bergetto* did:
And though my fault to him were meerely chance,
Yet humbly I submit me to your Grace,
To doe with mee as you please.

 Car. Rise vp *Grimaldi*,
You Cittizens of *Parma*, if you seeke
For Iustice; Know as *Nuntio* from the Pope,
For this offence I here receiue *Grimaldi*
Into his holinesse protection.
Hee is no Common man, but nobly borne;
Of Princes blood, though you Sir *Florio*,
Thought him to meane a husband for your daughter
If more you seeke for, you must goe to *Rome*,
For hee shall thither; learne more wit for shame.
Bury your dead---away *Grimaldi*---leaue 'em. *Ex. Car. & Gri.*

 Do. Is this a Church-mans voyce? dwels *Iustice* here?

 Flo. *Iustice* is fledd to Heauen and comes no neerer.
Soranzo, was't for him? O Impudence!
Had he the face to speake it, and not blush?
Come, come *Donado*, there's no helpe in this,
When *Cardinals* thinke murder's not amisse,
Great men may doe there wills, we must obey,
But Heauen will iudge them for't auother day. *Exeunt.*

  Actus

Actus Quartus.

A Banquet.   Hoboyes.

Enter the Fryar, Giouanni, Annabella, Philotis, Soranzo, Donado, Florio, Richardetto, Putana *and* Vasques.

F y. THese holy rights perform'd, now take your times,
To spend the remnant of the day in Feast;
Such fit repasts are pleasing to the Saints
Who are your guests, though not with mortall eyes
To be beheld; long prosper in this day
You happy Couple, to each others ioy:

Soran. Father, your prayer is heard, the hand of goodnesse
Hath beene a sheild for me against my death;
And more to blesse me, hath enricht my life
With this most precious Iewell; such a prize
As Earth hath not another like to this.
Cheere vp my Loue, and Gentlemen, my Friends,
Reioyce with mee in mirth, this day wee'le crowne
With lusty Cups to *Annabella's* health.

Gio. Oh Torture, were the marriage yet vndone,   *Aside.*
Ere I'de endure this sight, to see my Loue
Clipt by another, I would dare Confusion,
And stand the horrour of ten thousand deaths.

Vas. Are you not well Sir?

Gio. Prethee fellow wayte,
I neede not thy officious diligence.

Flo. Signior *Donado,* come you must forget
Your late mishaps, and drowne your cares in wine.

So an. Vasques?

Vas. My Lord.

Soran. Reach me that weighty bowle,
Here brother *Giouanni,* here's to you,

Your

Your turne comes next, though now a Batchelour,
Here's to your sisters happinesse and mine.

Gio. I cannot drinke.

Soran. What?

Gio. 'Twill indeede offend me.

Anna. Pray, doe not vrge him if hee be not willing.

Flo. How now, what noyse is this?

Vas. O sir, I had forgot to tell you; certaine young Maidens of *Parma* in honour to Madam *Annabella's* marriage, haue sent their loues to her in a Masque, for which they humbly craue your patience and silence.

Soran. Wee are much bound to them, so much the more as it comes vnexpected; guide them in.

Hoboyes.

Enter Hippolita *and Ladies in white Roabes with Garlands of Willowes.*

Musicke and a Daunce.   *Dance.*

Soran. Thanks louely Virgins, now might wee but know
To whom wee haue beene beholding for this loue,
Wee shall acknowledge it.

Hip. Yes, you shall know,
What thinke you now?

Omnes Hippolita?

Hip. 'Tis shee,
Bee not amaz'd; nor blush young louely Bride,
I come not to defraud you of your man,
'Tis now no time to reckon vp the talke
What *Parma* long hath rumour'd of vs both,
Let rash report run on; the breath that vents it
Will (like a bubble) breake it selfe at last.
But now to you *Sweet Creature*, lend's your hand,
Perhaps it hath beene said, that I would claime
Some interest in *Soranzo*, now your Lord,
What I haue right to doe, his soule knowes best:
But in my duty to your Noble worth,
Sweete *Annabella*, and my care of you,

      Here

··· take *Soranzo*, take this hand from me,
I'le once more ioyne, what by the holy Church
Is finish't and allow'd ; haue I done well?

   Soran. You haue too much ingag'd vs.

   Hip. One thing more
That you may know my single charity,
Freely I here remit all interest
I ere could clayme ; and giue you backe your vowes,
And to confirm't, reach me a Cup of wine
My Lord *Soranzo*, in this draught I drinke,
Long rest t'ee ——   looke to it *Vasques.*

   Vas. Feare nothing——   *He giues her a poysond Cup.*

   Soran. *Hippolita*, I thanke you, and will pledge (*She drinks.*
This happy Vnion as another life,
Wine there.

   Vas. You shall haue none, neither shall you pledge her.

   Hip. How !

   Vas. Know now Mistresse shee deuill, your owne mischieuous
Hath kild you, I must not marry you.   (*treachery*

   Hip. Villaine.

   Omnes. What's the matter ?

   Vas. Foolish woeman, thou art now like a Fire-brand, that
hath kindled others and burnt thy selfe ; *Troppo sperar niganna,*
thy vaine hope hath deceiued thee, thou art but dead, if thou
hast any grace, pray.

   Hip. Monster.

   Vas. Dye in charity for shame,
This thing of malice, this woman had priuately corrupted mee
with promise of malice, vnder this politique reconciliation to
to poyson my Lord, whiles shee might laugh at his Confusion
on his marriage-day ; I promis'd her faire, but I knew what my
reward should haue beene, and would willingly haue spar'd her
life, but that I was acquainted with the danger of her disposition, and now haue fitted her a iust payment in her owne coyne,
there shee is, shee hath yet —— —— and end thy dayes in
peace vild woman; as for life there's no hope, thinke not on't.

   Omnes. Wonderfull Iustice !

                                Richard.

Richard. Heauen thou art righteous.

Hip. O 'tis true,
I feele my minute comming, had that slaue
Kept promise, (o my torment) thou this houre
Had'ft dyed *Soranzo*---heate aboue hell fire---
Yet ere I paffe away-----Cruell, cruell flames---
Take here my curfe amongft you; may thy bed
Of marriage be a racke vnto thy heart,
Burne blood and boyle in Vengeance----o my heart,
My Flame's intolerable-----maift thou liue
To father Baftards, may her wombe bring forth
Monfters, and dye together in your finnes
Hated, fcorn'd and vnpittied--- oh---oh---   *Dyes.*

Flo: Was e're fo vild a Creature?
Richard. Here's the end
Of luft and pride.   *Anna.* It is a fearefull fight.

Soran. *Vafques*, I know thee now a trufty feruant,
And neuer will forget thee----come *My Loue*,
Wee'le home, and thanke the Heauens for this efcape,
Father and Friends, wee muft breake vp this mirth,
It is too fad a Feaft.

Do. Beare hence the body.
Fry. Here's an ominous change,
Marke this my *Gionani*, and take heed,
I feare the euent; that marriage feldome's good,
Where the bride-banquet fo begins in blood. *Exeunt.*
Enter Richardetto *and* Philotis.

Richard. My wretched wife more wretched in her fhame
Then in her wrongs to me, hath hath paid too foone
The forfeit of her modefty and life.
And I am fure (my Neece) though vengeance houer,
Keeping aloofe yet from *Soranzo's* fall,
Yet hee will fall, and finke with his owne weight.
I need not (now my heart perfwades me fo)
To further his confufion; there is one
Aboue begins to worke, for as I heare,
Debate's already twixt his wife and him,

Thicken

Thicken and run to head; shee (as 'tis sayd)
Sleightens his loue, and he abandons hers
Much talke I heare, since things goe thus (my Neece)
In tender loue and pitty of your youth,
My counsell is, that you should free your yeeres
From hazard of these woes; by flying hence
To faire *Cremona*, there to vow your soule
In holinesse a holy Votaresse,
Leaue me to see the end of these extreames
All humane worldly courses are vneuen,
No life is blessed but the way to Heauen.

    Phi. Vnkle, shall I resolue to be a Nun?

  Richard. I gentle Neece, and in your hourely prayers
Remember me your poore, vnhappy Vnkle;
Hie to *Cremona* now, as Fortune leades,
Your home, your cloyster, your best Friends, your beades,
Your chast an I single life shall crowne your Birth,
Who dyes a Virgine, liue a Saint on earth.

    Phi. Then farwell world, and worldly thoughts adeiu,
Welcome chast vowes, my selfe I yeeld to you.   *Exeunt.*

     Enter Soranzo *vnbrac't, and* Annabella *dragg'd in.*

   Soran. Come strumpet, famous whoore, were euery drop
Of blood that runs in thy adulterous veynes
A life, this Sword, (dost see't) should in one blowe
Confound them all, Harlot, rare, notable Harlot,
That with thy brazen face maintainst thy sinne.
Was there no man in *Parma* to be bawd
To your loose cunning whoredome else but I?
Must your hot ytch and plurisie of lust,
The heyday of your luxury be fedd
Vp to a surfeite, and could none but I
Be pickt out to be cloake to your close tricks,
Your belly-sports? Now I must be the Dad
To all that gallymaufrey that's stuft
In thy Corrupted bastard-bearing wombe,

                                        Say,

Shey, must I?

Anna. Beastly man, why 'tis thy fate:
I sued not to thee, for, but that I thought
Your *Ouer-louing Lordship* would haue runne
Madd on denyall, had yee lent me time,
I would haue told 'ee in what case I was,
But you would needes be doing.

Soran. Whore of whores!
Dar'st thou tell mee this?

Anna. O yes, why not?
You were deceiu'd in mee; 'twas not for loue
I chose you, but for honour; yet know this,
Would you be patient yet, and hide your shame,
I'de see whether I could loue you.

Soran. Excellent Queane!
Why art thou not with Child?

Anna. What needs all this,
When 'tis superfluous? I confesse I am.

Soran. Tell mee by whome.

Anna. Soft sir, 'twas not in my bargaine.
Yet somewhat sir to stay your longing stomacke
I'me content t'acquaint you with; *The man,*
The more then *Man* that got this sprightly Boy,
(For 'tis a Boy that for glory sir,
Your heyre shalbe a Sonne.)

Soran. Damnable Monster.

Anna. Nay and you will not heare, I'le speake no more.

Soran. Yes speake, and speake thy last.

Anna. A match, a match;
This *Noble Creature* was in euery part
So angell-like, so glorious, that a woeman,
Who had not beene but human as was I,
Would haue kneel'd to him, and haue beg'd for loue.
You, why you are not worthy once to name
His name without true worship, or indeede,
Vnlesse you kneel'd, to heare another name him.

Soran. What was hee cal'd?

H

Anna.

Anna. Wee are not come to that,
Let it ſuffice, that you ſhall haue the glory,
To *Father* what ſo *Braue a Father got.*
In briefe, had not this chance, falne out as 't doth,
I neuer had beene troubled with a thought
That you had beene *a Creature* ; but for marriage,
I ſcarce dreame yet of that.

 Soran. Tell me his name.

 Anna. Alas, alas, there's all
Will you beleeue?

 Soran. What?

 Anna. You ſhall neuer know.   *Soran.* How!

 Anna. Neuer,
If you doe, let mee be curſt.

 Soran. Not know it, Strumpet, I'le ripp vp thy heart,
And finde it there.

 Anna. Doe, doe.

 Soran. And with my teeth,
Teare the prodigious leacher joynt by ioynt.

 Anna. Ha, ha, ha, the man's merry.

 Soran. Do'ſt thou laugh?
Come *Whore,* tell mee your louer, or by Truth
I'le hew thy fleſh to ſhreds ; who is 't

 Anna. *Che morte pluis dolce che morire per amore.*   *ſings.*

 Soran. Thus will I pull thy hayre, and thus I'le drag
Thy luſt be-leapred body through the duſt.
Yet tell his name.

 Anna. *No endo in gratia Lei morire ſenza dolore.*   *ſings*

 Soran. Doſt thou Triumph? the Treaſure of the Earth
Shall not redeeme thee, were there kneeling Kings,
Did begge thy life, or Angells did come downe
To plead in teares; yet ſhould not all preuayle
Againſt my rage ; do'ſt thou not tremble yet?

 Anna. At what? to dye; No, be a *Gallant hang-man*
I dare thee to the worſt, ſtrike, and ſtrike home;
leaue reuenge behind, and thou ſhalt feel't.

            Soran,

Soran. Yet tell mee ere thou dyest, and tell mee truely,
Knowes thy old Father this?   *Anna.* No by my life.

Soran. Wilt thou confesse, and I will spare thy life?

Anna. My life? I will not buy my life so deare.

Soran. I will not slacke my Vengeance.

Enter Vasques.

Vas. What d'ee meane Sir?

Soran. Forbeare *Vasques*, such a damned *Whore*
Deserues no pitty.

Vas. Now the gods forefend!
And wud you be her executioner, and kill her in your rage too?
O'twere most vn-manlike; shee is your wife, what faults hath
beene done by her before she married you, were not against you;
alas *Poore Lady*, what hath shee committed, which any Lady
in *Italy* in the like case would not? Sir, you must be ru'ed by
your reason, and not by your fury, that were vnhumane and
beastly.

Soran. Shee shall not liue.

Vas. Come shee must; you would haue her confesse the Au-
thors of her present misfortunes I warrant'ee, 'tis an vnconscio-
nable demand, and shee should loose the estimation that I (for
my part) hold of her worth, if shee had done it; why sir you
ought not of all men liuing to know it: good sir bee reconciled,
elas good gentlewoman.

Anna. Pish, doe not beg for mee, I prize my life
As nothing; if *The man* will needs bee madd,
Why let him take it.

Soran. *Vasques,* hear'st thou this?

Vas. Yes, and commend her for it; in this shee shews the no-
blenesse of a gallant spirit, and beshrew my heart, but it becomes
her rarely————Sir, in any case smother your reuenge; leaue
the senting out your wrongs to mee, bee rul'd as you respect
hour honour, or you marr all—,—Sir, if euer my seruice were of
any Credit with you, be not so violent in your distractions: you
are married now; what a tryumph might the report of this giue
to other neglected Sutors, 'tis as manlike to beare extremities,
as godlike to forgiue.

H 2

Soran.

Soran. O *Vasques, Vasques,* in this peece of flesh,
This faithlesse face of hers, had I layd vp
The treasure of my heart; hadst thou beene vertuous
(Faire wicked woeman) not the matchlesse ioyes
Of Life it selfe had made mee wish to liue
With any Saint but thee; *Deceitfull Creature,*
How hast thou mock't my hopes, and in the shame
Of thy lewd wombe, euen buried mee aliue?
I did too dearely loue thee.

   Vas. This is well;
Follow this temper with some passion,
Bee briefe and mouing, 'tis for the purpose.   *Aside.*

   Soran. Be witnesse to my words thy soule and thoughts,
And tell mee didst not thinke that in my heart,
I did too superstitiously adore thee.

   Anna. I must confesse, I know you lou'd mee well.

   Soran. And wouldst thou vse mee thus? O *Annabella,*
Bee thus assur'd, whatsoe're the Villaine was,
That thus hath tempted thee to *This disgrace,*
Well hee might lust, but neuer lou'd like mee:
Hee doated on the picture that hung out
Vpon thy cheekes, to pleafe his humourous eye;
Not on the part I lou'd, which was thy heart,
And as I thought, thy Vertues.

   Anna. O my Lord!
These words wound deeper then your Sword could do.

   Vas. Let mee not euer take comfort, but I begin to weepe my
selfe, so much I pitty him; why *Madam* I knew when his rage
was ouer-past, what it would come to.

   Soran. Forgiue mee *Annabella,* though thy youth
Hath tempted thee aboue thy strength to folly,
Yet will not I forget what I should bee,
And what I am, a husband; in that name
Is hid Deuinity; if I doe finde
That thou wilt yet be true, here I remit
all former faults, and take thee to my bosome.

   Vas. By my troth, and that's a poynt of noble charity.

                              Anna.

Anna. Sir on my knees——

Soran. Riſe vp, you ſhall not kneele,
Get you to your chamber, ſee you make no ſhow
Of alteration, I le be with you ſtreight;
My reaſon tells mee now, that *'Tis as common*
To erre in frailty as to bee a woeman.
Goe to your chamber.   *Exit* Anna.

   Vaſ. So, this was ſomewhat to the matter; what doe you
thinke of your heauen of happineſſe now ſir?

   Soran. I carry hell about mee, all my blood
Is fir'd in ſwift reuenge.

   Vaſ. That may bee, but know yoo how, or on whom? alas,
to marry a great woeman, being made great in the ſtocke to your
hand, is a vſuall ſport in theſe dayes; but to know what *Secret*
it was that haunted your *Cunny-berry*, there's the cunning.

   Soran. I'le make her tell her ſelfe, or——

   Vaſ. Or what? you muſt not doe ſo, let me yet perſwade your
ſufferance a little while, goe to her, vſe her mildly, winne her if
it be poſſible to a Voluntary, to a weeping tune; for the reſt, if
all hitt, I will not miſſe my marke; pray ſir goe in, the next news
I tell you ſhall be wonders.

   Soran. Delay in vengeance giues a heauyer blow.   *Exit.*

   Vaſ. Ah ſirrah, here's worke for the nonce; I had a ſuſpici-
on of a bad matter in my head a pretty whiles agoe; but after *My*
Madams ſcuruy lookes here at home, her waſpiſh peruerſneſſe,
and loud fault-finding, then I remembred the Prouerbe, that
where Hens crowe, and Cocks hold their peace, there are ſorry
houſes; sfoot, if the lower parts of a *Shee-taylers Cunning,* can
couer ſuch a ſwelling in the ſtomacke, I'le neuer blame a falſe
ſtich in a ſhoe whiles I liue againe; vp and vp ſo quicke? and ſo
quickly too? 'twere a fine policy to learue by whom this muſt
be knowne: and I haue thought on't———here's the way or
none——— what crying old Miſtreſſe! alas, alas, I cannot blame
'ee, wee haue a Lord, Heauen helpe vs, is ſo madde as the devill
himſelfe, the more ſhame for him.

                         Enter Putana.

   Put. O *Vaſques,* that euer I was borne to ſee this day,

D'th hee vse thee so too, sometimes *Vasques* ?

Vas. Mee? why hee makes a dogge of mee; but if some were of my minde, I know what wee would doe; as sure as I am an honest man, hee will goe neere to kill my Lady with vnkindnesse; say shee be with-child, is that such a matter for a young woeman of her yeeres, to be blam'd for?

Put. Alas good heart, it is against her will full sore.

Vas. I durst be sworne, all his madnesse is, for that shee will not confesse whose 'tis, which hee will know, and when he doth know it, I am so well acquainted with his humour, that hee will forget all streight; well I could wish, shee would in plaine termes tell all, for that's the way indeed.

Put. Doe you thinke so?

Vas. Fo, I know't; prouided that hee did not winne her to't by force, hee was once in a mind, that you could tell, and ment to haue wrung it out of you, but I somewhat pacified him for that; yet sure you know a great deale.

Put. Heauen forgiue vs all, I know a little *Vasques*.

Vas. Why should you not? who else should? vpon my Con-science shee loues you dearely, and you would not betray her to any affliction for the world.

Put. Not for all the world by my Faith and troth *Vasques*.

Vas. 'Twere pitty of your life if you should, but *In this* you should both releiue her present discomforts, pacifie my Lord, and gaine your selfe euerlasting loue and preferment.

Put. Do'st thinke so *Vasques* ?

Vas. Nay I know't; sure 'twas some neere and entire friend.

Put. 'Twas a deare friend indeed; but——

Vas. But what? feare not to name him; my life betweene you and danger; faith I thinke 'twas no base Fellow.

Put. Thou wilt stand betweene mee and harme?

Vas. V'ds pitty, what else; you shalbe rewarded too; trust me.

Put. 'Twas euen no worse then her owne brother.

Vas. Her brother *Giouanni* I warrant 'ee?

Put. Euen hee *Vasques*; as braue a Gentleman as euer kist faire Lady.; O they loue most perpetually.

Vas. A braue Gentleman indeed; why therein I Commend

her

her choyce----better and better-----you are sure 'twas hee ?

Put. Sure; and you fhall'fee hee will not be long from her too.

Vaf. He were to blame if he would : but may I beleeue thee?

Put. Beleeue mee ! why do'ft thinke I am a Turke or a Iew? no *Vafques*, I haue knowne their dealings too long to belye them now.

Vaf. Where are you ? there within firs ?

                    Enter Bandetti.

Put. How now, what are thefe ?

Vaf. You fhall know prefently,

Come firs, take mee *This old Damnable hagge,*

Gag her inftantly, and put out her eyes, quickly, quickly.

Put. Vafques, Vafques.

Vaf. Gag her I fay, sfoot d'ee fuffer her to prate ? what d'ee fumble about ? let mee come to her , I'le helpe your old gums, you Toad-bellied bitch ; firs, carry her clofely into the Coale-houfe, and put out her eyes inftantly ; if fhee roares, flitt her nofe ; d'ee heare, bee fpeedy and fure. Why this is excellent and aboue expectation.   *Exit with* Putana.

Her owne brother ? O horrible-! to what a height of liberty in damnation hath the Deuill trayn'd our age, her Brother, well ; there's yet but a beginning, I muft to my Lord, and tutor him better in his points of vengeance ; now I fee how a fmooth tale goes beyond a fmooth tayle, but foft,---

what thing comes next ?   *Enter* Giouanni.

Giouanni ! as i would wifh ; my beleefe is ftrengthned,

'Tis as firme as Winter and Summer.

Gio. Where's my Sifter ?

Vaf. Troubled with a new ficknes my Lord, fhe's fomwhat ill,

Gio. Tooke too much of the flefh I beleeue.

Vaf. Troth fir and you I thinke haue e'ne hitt it,

But *My vertuous Lady.*

Gio. Where's fhee ?

Vaf. In her chamber; pleafe you vifit her; fhe is alone, your li-berality hath doubly made me your feruant, and euer fhal euer--- *Exit* Gio.

Sir, I am made a man, I haue plyed my Cure with cunning *Enter* So-

                            and ranzo.

and succeſſe, I beſeech you let's be priuate.

Soran. My Ladyes brother's come, now hee'le know all.

Vaſ. Let him know't, I haue made ſome of them faſt enough,
How haue you delt with my Lady?

Soran- Gently, as thou haſt counſail'd; O my ſoule
Runs circular in ſorrow for reuenge,
But *Vaſques*, thou ſhalt know----

Vaſ. Nay, I will know no more; for now comes your turne
to know; I would not talke ſo openly with you: Let my young
Maiſter take time enough, and goe at pleaſure; hee is ſold to
death, and the Deuill ſhall not ranſome him, Sir I beſeech you,
your priuacy.

Soran. No Conqueſt can gayne glory of my feare.   *Exit.*

Actus Quintus.

Enter Annabella *aboue.*

Anna. Pleaſures farwell, and all yee thriftleſſe minutes,
  Wherein *Falſe ioyes* haue ſpun a weary life,
To theſe my Fortunes now I take my leaue.
Thou *Precious Time*, that ſwiftly rid'ſt in poaſt
Ouer the world, to finiſh vp the race
Of my laſt fate; here ſtay thy reſtleſſe courſe,
And beare to Ages that are yet vnborne,
A wretched woefull woemans *Tragedy*,
My Conſcience now ſtands vp againſt my luſt
With diſpoſitions charectred in guilt,   *Enter* Fryar.
And tells mee I am loſt: *Now* I confeſſe,
Beauty that cloathes the out-ſide of the face,
Is curſed if it be not cloath'd with grace:
Here like a Turtle (mew'd vp in a Cage)
Vn-mated, I conuerſe with Ayre and walls,
And deſcant on my vild vnhappineſſe.
O *Giouanni*, that haſt had the ſpoyle

Of thine owne vertues and my modest fame,
Would thou hadst beene lesse subiect to those Stars
That luckelesse raign'd at my Natiuity :
O would the scourge due to my blacke offence
Might passe from thee, that *I alone* might feele
The torment of an vncontrouled flame.

   Fry. What's this I heare?

   Anna. That man, that *Blessed Fryar,*
Who ioyn'd in Ceremoniall knot my hand
To him whose wife I now am ; told mee oft,
I troad the path to death, and shewed mee how.
But they who sleepe in Lethargies of Lust
Hugge their confusion; making Heauen vniust,
And so did I.

   Fry. Here's Musicke to the soule.

   Anna. Forgiue mee my *Good Genius,* and this once
Be helpfull to my ends ; Let some good man
Passe this way, to whose trust I may commit
This paper double lin'd with teares and blood :
Which being granted ; here I sadly vow
Repentance, and a leauing of that life
I long haue dyed in.

   Fry. Lady, Heauen hath heard you,
And hath by prouidence ordain'd, that I
should be his Minister for your behoofe.

   Anna. Ha, what are you?

   Fry. Your brothers friend the Fryar ;
Glad in my soule that I haue liu'd to heare
This free confession twixt your peace and you,
What would you or to whom? feare not to speake.

   Anna. Is Heauen so bountifull? then I haue found
More fauour then I hop'd ; here *Holy man*——— *Throwes a letter.*
Commend mee to my Brother giue him that,
That Letter ; bid him read it and repent,
Tell him that I (imprison'd in my chamber,
Bard of all company, euen of *My Guardian,*
Who giues me cause of much suspect) haue time

I

          To

To blush at what hath past : bidd him be wise,
And not beleeue the Friendship of my Lord,
I feare much more then I can speake; *Good father,*
The place is dangerous, and spyes are busie;
I must breake off ——————   you'le doe't?

   Fry. Be sure I will;
And fly with speede —— my blessing euer rest
With thee my daughter, liue to dye more blessed.   *Exit* Fry.

   Anna. Thanks to the heauens, who haue prolong'd my breath
To this good vse : Now I can welcome Death.   *Exit.*

        Enter Soranzo *and* Vasques.

   Vas. Am I to be beleeu'd now?
First, marry a strumpet that cast her selfe away vpon you but to
laugh at your hornes? to feast on your disgrace, riott in your vex-
ations, cuckold you in your bride-bed, waste your estate vpon
Panders and Bawds?

   Soran. No more, I say no more.

   Vas. A Cuckold is a goodly tame beast my Lord.

   Soran. I am resolu'd; vrge not another word;
My thoughts are great, and all as resolute
As thunder; in meane time I'le cause our Lady
To decke her selfe in all her bridall Robes,
Kisse her, and fold her gently in my armes,
Begone; yet heare you, are the *Bandetti* ready
To waite in Ambush?

   Vas. Good Sir, trouble not your selfe about other busines, then
your owne resolution; remember that time lost cannot be recal'd.

   Soran. With all the cunning words thou canst, inuite
The States of *Parma* to my Birth-dayes feast,
Haste to my *Brother rivall* and his Father,
Entreate them gently, bidd them not to fayle,
Bee speedy and returne.

   Vas. Let not your pitty betray you, till my comming backe,
Thinke vpon *Incest* and *Cuckoldry.*

   Soran. Reuenge is all the Ambition I aspire,
To that I'le clime or fall; my blood's on fire.   *Exeunt.*
                                   Enter

Enter Giouanni.

Gio. *Buſe opinion* is an idle Foole,
That as a Schoole-rod keepes a child in awe,
Frights the vnexperienc't temper of the mind :
So did it mee ; who ere *My precious Siſter*
Was married, thought all taſt of loue would dye
In ſuch a Contract ; but I finde no change
Of pleaſure in this formall law of ſports.
Shee is ſtill one to mee, and euery kiſſe
As ſweet, and as delicious as the firſt
I reap't ; when yet the priuiledge of youth
Intitled her *a Virgine :* O the glory
Of two vnited hearts like hers and mine !
Let *Poaring booke-men* dreame of other worlds,
My world, and all of happineſſe is here,
And I'de not change it for the beſt to come,
A life of pleaſure is Elyzeum.   *Enter* Fryar.
Father, you enter on the *Iubile*
Of my retyr'd delights ; Now I can tell you,
The hell you oft haue prompted, is nought elſe
But ſlauiſh and fond ſuperſtitious feare ;
And I could proue it too——
    Fry. Thy blindneſſe ſlayes thee,
Looke there, 'tis writt to thee.   *Giues the*
    Gio. From whom ?   *Letter.*
    Fry. Vnrip the ſeales and ſee :
The blood's yet ſeething hot, that will anon
Be frozen harder then congeal'd Corrall.
Why d'ee change colour ſonne ?
    Gio. Fore Heauen you make
Some petty Deuill factor 'twixt my loue
And your relligion-masked ſorceries.
Where had you this ?
    Fry. Thy Conſcience youth is fear'd,
Elſe thou wouldſt ſtoope to warning.
    Gio. 'Tis her hand,

I know't ; and 'tis all written in her blood.
She writes I know not what; Death? I'le not feare
An armed thunder-bolt aym'd at my heart;
Shee writes wee are discouered, pox on dreames
Of lowe faint-hearted Cowardise ; discouered ?
The Deuill wee are ; which way is't possible ?
Are wee growne Traytours to our owne delights ?
Confusion take such dotage, 'tis but forg'd;
This is your peeuish chattering weake old man,
Now sir, what newes bring you ?

          Enter Vasques.

  Vas. My Lord, according to his yearely custome keeping this
day a Feast in honour of his Birth-day, by mee, inuites you thither ; your worthy Father with the Popes reuerend *Nuntio*, and
other Magnifico's of *Parma*, haue promis'd their presence, will
please you to be of the number ?

  Gio. Yes, tell them I dare come.

  Vas. Dare come?

  Gio. So I sayd ; and tell him more I will come.

  Vas. These words are strange to mee.

  Gio. Say I will come.

  Vas. You will not misse?

  Gio. Yet more, I'le come ; sir, are you answer'd?

  Vas. So I'le say——my seruice to you.   *Exit Vas.*

  Fry. You will not goe I trust.

  Gio. Not goe? for what ?

  Fry. O doe not goe, this feast (I'le gage my life)
Is but a plot to trayne you to your ruine,
Be rul'd, you sha'not goe.

  Gio. Not goe? stood Death
Threatning his armies of confounding plagues,
With hoasts of dangers hot as blazing Starrs,
I would be there ; not goe? yes and resolue
To strike as deepe in slaughter as they all.
For I will goe.

  Fry. Goe where thou wilt, I see
The wildnesse of thy Fate drawes to an end,

                            To

To a bad fearefull end; I must not stay
To know thy fall, backe to *Bononia* I
With speed will haste, and shun this comming blowe,
Parma farwell, would I had neuer knowne thee,
Or ought of thine; well *Youngman,* since no prayer
Can make thee safe, I leaue thee to despayre.   *Exit Fry.*
    Despaire or tortures of a thousand hells
All's one to mee; I haue set vp my rest.
Now, now, worke serious thoughts on banefull plots,
Be all a man my soule; let not the Curse
Of old prescription rent from mee the gall
Of Courage, which inrolls a glorious death.
If I must totter like a well-growne Oake,
Some vnder shrubs shall in my weighty fall
Be crusht to splitts: with mee they all shall perish.   *Exit.*

     Enter Soranzo, Vasques, *and* Bandetti.

Soran. You will not fayle, or shrinke in the attempt?
  Vas. I will vndertake for their parts; be sure my Maisters to
be bloody enough, and as vnmercifull, as if you were praying
vpon a rich booty on the very Mountaines of *Liguria*; for your
pardons trust to my Lord; but for reward you shall trust none,
but your owne pockets.
  Ban. omnes. Wee'le make a murther.
  Soran. Here's gold, here's more; want nothing; what you do
is noble, and an act of braue reuenge.
I'le make yee rich *Bandetti* and all Free.
  Omnes. Liberty, liberty.
  Vas. Hold, take euery man a Vizard; when yee are with-
drawne, keepe as much silence as you can possibly; you know
the watch-word, till which be spoken, moue not, but when you
heare *that,* rush in like a stormy-flood; I neede not instruct yee
in your owne profession.
  Omnes. No, no, no.
  Vas. In then, your ends are profit and preferment---away.   *Exit Ban-*
  Soran. The guests will all come *Vasques*?   *detti.*
  Vas. Yes sir,

         and

and now let me a little edge your resolution ;
you see nothing is vnready to this *Great worke*, but a great mind
in you ; Call to your remembrance your disgraces, your losse of
Honour, *Hippolita's* blood ; and arme your courage in your owne
wrongs, so shall you best right those wrongs in vengeance
which you may truely call *Your owne*.

Soran. 'Tis well ; the lesse I speake, the more I burne,
and bloed shall quecch that flame.

Vas. Now you begin to turne Italian, this beside, when my
young *Incest-monger* comes, hee wilbe sharpe set on his old bitt :
giue him time enough, let him haue your Chamber and bed at liberty ; let my *Hot Hare* haue law ere he be hunted to his death,
that if it be possible, hee may poast to Hell in the very Act of his
damnation.

Soran. It shall be so ; and see as wee would wish,
Hee comes himselfe first ; welcome my *Much-lou'd brother*,
Now I perceiue you honour me ; y'are welcome,
But where's my father ?

Gio. With the other States,
Attending on the *Nuntio* of the Pope
To waite vpon him hither ; how's my sister ?

Soran. Like a good huswife, scarcely ready yet,
Y'are best walke to her chamber.

Gio. If you will.

Soran. I must expect my honourable Friends,
Good brother get her forth.

Gio. You are busie Sir. — *Exit* Giouanni.

Vas. Euen as the great Deuill himselfe would haue it, let him
goe and glut himselfe in his owne destruction ; harke, the *Nuntio*
is at hand ; good sir be ready to receiue him.

Enter. *Cardinall*, Florio, Donado, Richardetto *and Attendants*.

Soran. Most reuerend Lord, this grace hath made me proud,
That you vouchsafe my house ; I euer rest
Your humble seruant for this Noble Fauour.

Car. You are our Friend my Lord, his holinesse

K 1 Shall

Shall vnderſtand,how zealouſly you honour
Saint Peters Vicar in his ſubſtitute
Our ſpeciall loue to you.

Soran. Signiors to you
My welcome, and my euer beſt of thanks
For this ſo memorable courteſie,
Pleaſeth your Grace to walke neere?

Car. My Lord, wee come
To celebrate your Feaſt with Ciuill mirth,
As ancient cuſtome teacheth : wee will goe.

Soran. Attend his grace there,Signiors keepe your way.*Exeūt*

Enter Giouahni *and* Annabella *lying on a bed.*

Gio. What chang'd ſo ſoone ? hath your new ſprightly Lord
Feund out a tricke in night-games more then wee
Could know in our ſimplicity ? ha ! is't ſo ?
Or does the fitt come on you,to proue treacherous
To your paſt vowes and oathes ?

Anna. Why ſhould you jeaſt
At my Calamity,without all ſence
Of the approaching dangers you are in?

Gio. What danger's haife ſo great as thy reuolt?
Thou art a faithleſſe ſiſter,elſe thou know'ſt,
Malice, or any treachery beſide
Would ſtoope to my bent-browes; why I hold Fate
Claſp't in my fiſt, and could Command the Courſe
Of times eternall motion ; hadſt thou beene
One thought more ſteddy then an ebbing Sea.
And what? you'le now be honeſt, that's reſolu'd?

Anna. Brother, deare brother,know what I haue beene,
And know thatnow there's but a dyning time
Twixt vs and our Confuſion: let's not waſte
Theſe precious houres in vayne and vſeleſſe ſpeech.
Alas,theſe gay attyres were not put on
But to ſome end; this ſuddaine ſolemne Feaſt
Was not ordayn'd to riott in expence ;

I that haue now beene cham'bred here alone,
Bird of my Guardian, or of any elfe,
Am not for nothing at an inftant free'd
To frefh acceffe ; be not deceiu'd *My Brother*,
This Banquet is an harbinger of Death
To you and mee, refolue your felfe it is,
And be prepar'd to welcome it.

   Gio. Well then,
The *Schoole-men* teach that all this Globe of earth
Shalbe confum'd to afhes in a minute.

   Anna. So I haue read too.

   Gio. But 'twere fomewhat ftrange
To fee the Waters burne, could I beleeue
This might be true, I could beleeue afwell
There might be hell or Heauen.

   Anna. That's moft certaine.

   Gio A dreame, a dreame; elfe in this other world
Wee fhould know one another.

   Anna. So wee fhall.

   Gio. Haue you heard fo ?

   Anna. For certaine.

   Gio. But d'ee thinke,
That I fhall fee you there,
You looke on mee,
May wee kiffe one another,
Prate or laugh,
Or doe as wee doe here ?

   Anna. I know not that,
But good for the prefent, what d'ee meane
To free your felfe from danger ? fome way, thinke
How to efcape ; I'me fure the guefts are come.

   Gio. Looke vp, looke here ; what fee you in my face?

   Anna. Diftraction and a troubled Countenance.

   Gio. Death and a fwift repining wrath---yet looke,
What fee you in mine eyes ?

   Anna. Methinkes you weepe.

   Gio. I doe indeede; thefe are the funerall teares

Shedd

Shed on your graue, these furrowed vp my cheekes
When first I lou'd and knew not how to woe,
Faire *Annabella*, should I here repeate
The Story of my life, wee might loose time.
Be record all the spirits of the Ayre;
And all things else that are; that Day and Night,
Earely and late, the tribute which my heart
Hath paid to *Annabella's* sacred loue,
Hath been *these teares*, which are *her mourners now:*
Neuer till now did Nature doe her best,
To shew *a matchlesse beauty* to the world,
Which in an instant, ere it scarse was seene,
The jealous Destinies require againe.
Pray *Annabella*, pray; since wee must part,
Goe thou white in thy soule, to fill a Throne
Of Innocence and Sanctity in Heauen.
Pray, pray my Sister.
    Anna. Then I see your drift,
Yee blessed Angels, guard mee.
   Gio. So say I,
Kisse mee; if euer after times should heare
Of our fast-knit affections, though perhaps
The Lawes of *Conscience* and of *Ciuill vse*
May iustly blame vs, yet when they but know
Our loues, *That loue* will wipe away that rigour,
Which would in other *Incests* bee abhorr'd.
Giue mee your hand; how sweetely Life doth runne
In these well coloured veines! how constantly
These Palmes doe promise health! but I could chide
With Nature for this Cunning flattery,
Kisse mee againe———forgiue mee.
   Anna. With my heart.
   Gio. Farwell.
   Anna. Will you begone?
   Gio. Be darke bright Sunne,
And make this mid-dey night, that thy guilt rayes
May not behold a deed, will turne their splendour

K

More

More footy, then the *Poets* faigne their *Stix.*
One other kiffe my Sifter.

    Anna. What meanes this?

    Gio. To faue thy fame and kill thee in a kiffe.   *ftabs her.*
Thus dye, and dye by mee, and by my hand,
Reuenge is mine; Honour doth loue Command.

    Anna. Oh brother by your hand?

    Gio. When thou art dead
I'le giue my reafons for't; for to difpute
With thy (euen in thy death) moft louely beauty;
Would make mee ftagger to performe *this act*
Which I moft glory in.

    Anna. Forgiue him Heauen----and me my finnes, farwell:
Brother vnkind, vnkind---mercy great Heauen---oh--oh. *Dyes.*

    Gio. Shee's dead, alas good foule; *The haplesfe Fruite*
That in her wombe receiu'd its life from mee,
Hath had from mee a *Cradle and a Graue.*
I muft not dally, this fad Marriage-bed
In all her beft, bore her aliue and dead.
Soranzo thou haft mift thy ayme in this,
I haue preuented now thy reaching plots,
And kil'd a Loue, for whofe each drop of blood
I would haue pawn'd my heart; *Fayre Annabella,*
How ouer-glorious art thou in thy wounds,
Tryumphing ouer infamy and hate!
Shrinke not Couragious hand, ftand vp my heart,
And boldly act my laft, and greater part.   *Exit with the Body.*

                                  A Banquet.
Enter Cardinall, Florio, Donado, Soranzo, Richardetto, Vaf-
    ques *and attendants; They take their places.*

    Vaf. Remember Sir what you haue to do, be wife and refolute.

    Soran. Enough---my heart is fix't, pleafeth *Your Grace*
To tafte thefe Courfe Confections; though the vfe
Of fuch fet enterteyments more confifts
In Cuftome, then in Caufe; yet *Reuerend Sir,*
I am ftill made your feruant by your prefence.

Car. And wee your Friend.

Soran. But where's my Brother *Giouanni* ?

Enter Giouanni *with a heart vpon his Dagger.*

Gio. Here, here *Soranzo* ; trim'd in reeking blood,
That tryumphs ouer death ; proud in the spoyle
Of *Loue* and *Vengeance,* Fate or all the Powers
That guide the motions of Immortall Soules
Could not preuent mee.

Car. What meanes this ?

Flo. Sonne *Giouanni* ?

Soran. Shall I be forestall'd ?

Gio. Be not amaz'd : If your misgiuing hearts
Shrinke at an idle sight ; what bloodlesse Feare
Of Coward passion would haue ceaz'd your sences,
Had you beheld the *Rape of Life and Beauty*
Which I haue acted ? my sister, oh my sister.

Flo. Ha ! What of her ?

Gio. The Glory of my Deed
Darkned the mid-day Sunne, made Noone as Night.
You came to feast *My Lords* with dainty fare,
I came to feast too, but I dig'd for food
In a much richer Myne then Gold or Stone
Of any value ballanc't ; 'tis *a Heart*,
A Heart my Lords, in which is mine intomb'd,
Looke well vpon't ; d'ee know't ?

Vas. What strange ridle's this ?

Gio. 'Tis *Annabella's Heart,* 'tis ; why d'ee startle ?
I vow 'tis hers, this Daggers poynt plow'd vp
Her fruitefull wombe, and left to mee the fame
Of a most glorious executioner.

Flo. Why mad-man, art thy selfe ?

Gio. Yes Father, and that times to come may know,
How as my Fate I honoured my reuenge :
Lift Father, to your eares I will yeeld vp
How much I haue deseru'd to bee your sonne.

Flo. What is't thou say'st ?

Gio. Nine Moones haue had their changes,
Since I firft throughly view'd and truely lou'd
Your Daughter and *my Sifter.*

Flo. How ! alas my Lords, hee's a frantick mad-man !

Gio. Father no ;
For nine Moneths fpace, in fecret I enjoy'd
Sweete *Annabella's* fheetes ; Nine Moneths I liu'd
A happy Monarch of her heart and her,
Soranzo, thou know'ft this ; thy paler cheeke
Beares the Confounding print of thy difgrace,
For her too fruitfull wombe too foone bewray'd
The happy paffage of our ftolne delights,
And made her Mother to a Child vnborne.

Car. Inceftuous Villaine.

Flo. Oh his rage belyes him.

Gio. It does not, 'tis the Oracle of truth,
I vow it is fo.

Soran. I fhall burft with fury,
Bring the ftrumpet forth.

Vaf. I fhall Sir.   *Exit Vaf.*

Gio. Doe fir, haue you all no faith
To credit yet my Triumphs ? here I fweare
By all that you call facred, by the loue
I bore my *Annabella* whil ft fhe liu'd,
Thefe hands haue from her bofome ript *this heart.*
Is't true or no fir ?   *Enter Vaf.*

Vaf. 'Tis moft ftrangely true.

Flo. Curfed man—— haue I liu'd to———   *Dyes.*

Car. Hold vp *Florio,*
Monfter of Children, fee what thou haft done,
Broake thy old Fathers heart ; is none of you
Dares venter on him ?

Gio. Let 'em ; oh my Father,
How well his death becomes him in his griefes !
Why this was done with Courage ; now furuines
None of our houfe but I, guilt in the blood
Of a *Fayre fifter* and a *Haplesse Father.*

Soran. Inhamane scorne of men, hast thou a thought
T'out liue thy murthers?

Gio. Yes, I tell thee yes;
For in my fists I beare the twists of life,
Soranzo, see this heart which was thy wiues,
Thus I exchange it royally for thine,
And thus and thus, now braue reuenge is mine.

Vas. I cannot hold any longer; you sir, are you growne info-
lent in your butcheries? haue at you.　　　　　　　　*Fight.*

Gio. Come, I am arm'd to meete thee.

Vas. No, will it not be yet? if this will not, another shall,
Not yet; I shall fitt you anon——　　　　　　*Vengeance.*

Enter Bandetti.

Gio. Welcome, come more of you what e're you be,
I dare your worst————
Oh I can stand no longer, Feeble armes
Haue you so soone lost strength.

Vas. Now you are welcome Sir,
Away my Maisters, all is done,
Shift for your selues, your reward is your owne,
Shift for your selues.

Ban. Away, away.　　　　　　　　　*Exeunt* Bandetti.

Vas. How d'ee my Lord, see you this? how is't?

Soran. Dead; but in death well pleased, that I haue liu'd
To see my wrongs reueng'd on that *Blacke Deuill.*
O *Vasques,* to thy bosome let mee giue
My last of breath, let not that Lecher liue——oh　　*Dyes.*

Vas. The Reward of peace and rest be with him,
My euer dearest Lord and Maister.

Gio. Whose hand gaue mee this wound?

Vas. Mine Sir, I was your first man, haue you enough?

Gio. I thanke thee, thou hast done for me but what I would
haue else done on my selfe, ar't sure thy Lord is dead?

Vas. Oh Impudent slaue, as sure as I am sure to see the dye.

Car. Thinke on thy life and end, and call for mercy.

Gio. Mercy? why I haue found it in this *Iustice.*

Car. Striue yet to cry to Heauen.

K 3　　　　　　　　　　　　　　*Gio.*

Gio. Oh I bleed fast,

Death, thou art a guest long look't for, I embrace
Thee and thy wounds; oh my last minute comes.
Where e're I goe, let mee enioy this grace,
Freely to view *My Annabella's face.*   *Dyes.*

Do. Strange Miracle of Iustice!

Car. Rayse vp the Citty, wee shall be murdered all,

Vas. You neede not feare, you shall not; this strange taske being ended, I haue paid the Duty to the Sonne, which I haue vowed to the Father.

Car. Speake wretched Villaine, what incarnate Feind
Hath led thee on to this?

Vas. Honesty, and pitty of my Maisters wrongs; for know *My Lord*, I am by birth *a Spaniard*, brought forth my Countrey in my youth by Lord *Soranzo's* Father; whom whil'st he liued, I seru'd faithfully; since whose death I haue beene to this man, as I was to him; what I haue done was duty, and I repent nothing, but that the losse of my life had not ransom'd his.

Car. Say Fellow, know'st thou any yet vnnam'd
Of Counsell in this Incest?

Vas. Yes, an old woeman, sometimes *Guardian* to this murthered Lady.

Car. And what's become of her?

Vas. Within this Roome shee is, whose eyes after her confession I caus'd to be put out, but kept aliue, to confirme what from *Gionanni's* owne mouth you haue heard: now *My Lord*, what I haue done, you may Iudge of, and let your owne wisedome bee a iudge in your owne reason.

Car. Peace; First this woeman chiefe in these effects,
My sentence is, that forthwith shee be tane
Out of the Citty, for examples sake,
There to be burnt to ashes.

Do. 'Tis most iust.

Car. Be it your charge *Donado*, see it done.

Do. I shall.

Vas. What for mee? if death, 'tis welcome, I haue beene honest to the Sonne, as I was to the Father.

                                                            Car.

Car. Fellow, for thee; since what thou did'st, was done
Not for thy selfe, being no Italian,
Wee banish thee for euer, to depart
Within three dayes, in this wee doe dispense
With grounds of reason not of thine offence.

Vas. 'Tis well; this Conquest is mine, and I reioyce that a
Spaniard out-went an *Italian in reuenge.*   *Exit* Vas.

Car. Take vp these slaughtered bodies, see them buried,
And all the Gold and Iewells, or whatsoeuer,
Confiscate by the Canons of the Church,
Wee ceaze vpon to the Popes proper vse.

Richar. Your Graces pardon, thus long I liu'd disguis'd
To see the effect of *Pride and Lust* at once
Brought both to shamefull ends.

Car. What *Richardetto* whom wee thought for dead?

Do. Sir was it you——

Richar. Your friend,

Car. Wee shall haue time
To talke at large of all, but neuer yet
Incest and *Murther* haue so strangely met.
Of one so young, so rich in Natures store,
Who could not say, *'Tis pitty shee's a Whoore?*   *Exeunt.*

FINIS.

The generall Commendation deserued by the Actors, in
their Presentment of this Tragedy, may easily excuse such
few faults, as are escaped in the Printing : A common
charity may allow him the ability of spelling, whom a secure confidence assures that hee cannot ignorantly erre in
the Application of Sence.

Printed in the USA
CPSIA information can be obtained
at www.ICGtesting.com
LVHW010419300923
759528LV00010B/1169